Little girl speak

A path to healing your inner child

By:
Sarah Kacala

Little girl speak

By:
Sarah Kacala

1st Edition: 2020

Publisher Information
1st Edition: Debra McLain

ISBN: 9781656675576
Imprint: Independently published

$14.99

Dedication

This book is dedicated to the little girl inside me, whom I have grown to love so dearly. And to Ali Wilburn, whose support and compassion have been immeasurable. Without your wisdom and your light, my healing and this book, would not have been possible. Thank you from the depths of my soul, for helping me to step into my authenticity, with fierce abandon and courage.

And to every survivor: May you realize, that your light shines brighter than you could ever imagine, even on the darkest of nights. It is my mission, to help you find your fire and your voice once again, so that we can change the world, with our infinite wisdom and light.

Table of Contents

Introduction

Introduction

Hi. Allow me to introduce myself. My name is Sarah, and I am a survivor of childhood trauma. And chances are, if you're holding this book in your hands, that you are too. Chances are that you survived something that altered and changed your universe forever. You probably play host, to two different faces. The one that you show to the outside world, and the one that only you can see; the real you. People write to me all the time, and ask me: "How can I heal my inner child? And how do I know, if she's broken?" **How do I know, if she's broken?** If you're asking yourself that question, then you already know the answer…It's a very difficult thing, to accept the horror of what was done to us, so early on in our lives. It was a very difficult pill, for me to swallow. And it took a very tall glass of water, to choke it all down. But there is a certain power, in owning our stories; no matter how awful or heartbreaking they may be. There is a power, in accepting the things we cannot change. When we are able to do so, it makes room in our hearts, for us to turn our focus and attention to the things that we can. There are no quick fixes here. There are no shortcuts along the way. And no one wishes that there had been, more than me. I don't have any magic beans, or fairy dust up my sleeve. But I can assure you, that there is magic within yourself. And my goal in this book, is to help you uncover it. You are a well of wisdom. No one knows the inner workings of the human heart, better than a survivor.

People have been asking me for the last couple years, how I was able to get myself to the space where I now reside; this place where joy and peace have returned home, to my soul. It is a place where they used to exist freely, when I was a very small child. But when my safety was ripped right out from under me, joy and peace eluded me. They escaped through the crevices of my aching soul, and seeped right out of my fragile bones. I had assumed that they were gone forever; never to return home again. But I'm so very glad, that I was wrong about that. They did come back, but not on their own; not of their own free will. I had to fight to get them back. I had to work so hard, just to get back the things that never should have left me in the first place; things that were my God given right to hold tightly to, as a human being. Things that never should have been stolen from me. It doesn't seem fair, does it? And this space where I've come to dwell; this healed up heart that I've somehow grown into, has come to suit me well. But it took me a really long time to feel comfortable, inside this skin of mine. It took me what felt like a lifetime, to recover from my life. Every sharp turn, left me marred with bruises. Every unexpected spiral, left me pinned beneath fear, and an immense sense of shame. Now you're probably thinking to yourself: "Then why do it? Why go through all of that discomfort, and all of that pain?" But really, if you think about it, what other choice is there? I was trapped inside a mind prison. I was trapped inside a time machine, where I was seven years old inside my soul, with no hope of moving forward. What kind of a life is that? It's not really a life at all, is it? It's merely existing. Four years ago, I made a conscious decision to dedicate myself to my own healing; to restoring the inner workings, of my innermost soul. I knew that I had my work cut out for me. But I'm also a very determined human being. Survivors always are. No matter how weak you may feel in this moment, you are strong. And you were born, to rise. It is not frailty, that enabled you to make it this far. Heart beating; blood pumping through your veins. It is undeniable strength and courage that has enabled you to survive. And no matter how worn out and beat down you may feel right now, that strength is still very much alive, somewhere inside of you. And I'm making it my mission, to help you find it. To help you cultivate it, into a weapon. To help you use it, to free yourself from all of this weight you've been carrying around with you. You have an entire world's worth of deadweight on your shoulders that was never meant to be yours to carry. And we are going to unpack it, and study it together. We won't be tossing even one small piece into the trash can, unopened or unexplored. Everything in that huge backpack of yours, matters. It all matters, very much. I realized this, when I launched my blog. I am the author, of a blog. It is meant to empower and inspire other survivors like myself, to feel and to heal. And while each person's story may be a little bit different, I noticed many common threads, in the stories that were being shared with me. Common threads that mirrored my own journey. Feelings of severe shame and isolation. Loneliness, and a deep seated fear of never being believed, or loved ever again, if they were to disclose their stories of abuse to anyone close to them. When I first started receiving these emails through my blog, it cracked my heart wide open again, in a different way than it had been broken before. And I knew, that I had to do something more; something beyond those daily words of encouragement. I wanted to do more than just empower them, to continue surviving. I wanted to see them thrive again. I wanted to see them come alive, and heal, and grow. I wanted to witness survivors, turning into fierce warriors; embracing their authenticity and stepping into the lives of fullness and joy, that they were always meant to live. The more that people continued to ask me, how I managed to get to such a peaceful place in my heart, it had become crystal clear what I needed to do. I needed to write a book, about the process I went through. I needed to shed light, on what this journey of inner child healing has been for me. I needed to bring awareness, about how crucially important this process is for survivors. I needed to write a book, about what it looks like, and what it feels like, to heal your inner child; to literally grow her up inside of you, step by step. A guide of sorts. A pathway.

I wish that I could tell you that there is an exact science, to all of this healing; there isn't. And because each of us are a little bit different, we have all reacted to our trauma, in different ways. So while this process I'm going to share with you will work for the most part, as a healing framework due to our commonalities; you may have to tweak and further personalize a few of the steps along the way, to best suit your own healing journey. My goal within these pages is to try to explain the process I went through, in the hopes that you will be able to take nuggets of wisdom with you, on your own journey. But also, to possibly help you avoid some of the pitfalls that I fell into unknowingly, along the way. It's ok to be afraid of this healing process. It's not going to be easy. And I don't want to lie to you, and tell you that it will be. But what I can promise you, from the depths of my soul, is that it is one hundred percent worth it. It has been the hardest and best thing I have ever done, in my life. It is the greatest gift I've ever given to myself; my healing. So grab a seat, and settle in. Get in a comfortable spot. Curl up with a blanket, and keep reading. If you're still with me at this point, it means you're ready to embark on this journey with me. There will be days, when you may think you're changing your mind about that, but don't. Don't second guess your strength, and your tenacity, and your ability to heal and mend your shattered heart, and your broken sense of self. I will be with you every step of the way, as we unpack and uncover the truths that ravaged your soul, and cultivate the tools you will need to heal that inner child, and set her free. When you are finally able to release her from this prison inside of you, where she's never been able to grow up, you will feel a peace that you've never known before. This book won't cure you. It won't make everything rosy and wonderful, for the rest of your life. But I believe that the wisdom I've gained, from going through this process of falling, and failing miserably, and rising again; I believe that that wisdom can help you, to take the necessary steps, to begin to heal. Maybe you won't be so afraid of opening up that air tight heart of yours, to the possibility that healing can happen, if you know that you're not alone. I am here to tell you, that you are NOT alone. Your story is safe with me. Your tears are safe with me. Your heart is safe here. I know that healing your inner child, won't make everything in your life feel perfect again. I wasn't foolish enough to believe that about my own journey, and I'm certainly not going to peddle that pond scum to you. But it will make a big difference in your life. You will feel more at home, within yourself. You will find yourself holding onto hope more often, and for much longer periods of time. You will step into a truer, more authentic version of yourself. I know it's not perfect, but it's a really good start. If you can commit to taking this journey with me, I would be honored, to walk alongside you. It is truly my privilege. I want you to be able to move from surviving, into thriving. I know that I can't erase your painful past for you. Oh how I wish that I could. I may not be able to change your painful history. But it is my hope, that this book will open up a way, for you to be able to change the trajectory of your future. I may not be able to promise you that things will feel perfect in your life, after you're finished reading this book, and have applied these steps, in your healing process. But what I can assure you is that you will feel stronger, and you won't feel so alone, or misunderstood anymore. You will emerge from the ashes, feeling more FIERCE and more at peace, inside your own skin. And I think that's a really good place to start, don't you? So let's take a deep breath together, and begin. I'm going to start each chapter, with a quote from my blog. For those words are the very essence of who I've been, and they would come to form the bridge that would eventually lead me, where I was going.

"Of thin skin and draping bones, I am made. Self-hatred, my righteous accolade. I am deserving of nothing but this debt that I've paid. So I stand here in silence, as I long to be re-made. I vomit her shouts from the depths of my soul; this tortured little girl. She didn't ask for this. She didn't want to be different. She just wanted to feel safe and loved, in her world. She traded pillow fights, for sleepless nights. Lullabies with a man in her bed. No more laughter; only nightmares that kept her awake, suffocating all the dreams in her head. So don't stand there and tell me about moving forward. Do not speak to me, about how healing weaves through me, like an intricate thread. I don't want to be sitting here doing this work. Sometimes I think it would've been easier, if I had just ended up dead. So I turn up the music to drown out these demons, that grow louder and louder inside of my head. They scream and they shout as they're chanting my name; over and over and over again. You tell me to pick up these shards of glass, and to throw them as hard as I can. But nothing and no one can bring her back; that child inside of me, who's dead. He stole her smile. It took a while. For she held onto hope and believed. She thought that someone would rescue her soon; that somehow, someone would see. He tortured her body and twisted her mind, in ways that most humans would never survive. So she took all the shame, and turned it in on herself. She tried so hard to reshape her outsides; to look like someone else. She starved her body, until she couldn't breathe. Her only control was refusing to eat. She fell in love with the feeling, of her ribcage exposed. And why in the hell didn't anyone worry, about the frail little girl, who was always alone? The eight year old child who sat in the bathroom, with her fingers shoved down her throat. Purging her dinner, so that she could be thinner, so that he would stop raping her. She was a skeleton, in clothes. Those hours with him, were never about her body. Sex and power, seemed one and the same. I guess it blurs together, when you're dealing with a child. But she was never a fair opponent. And to her, it wasn't a game. Dizzy and blurry; she spent her life in a haze. Always longing to erase him. Always longing to be rid of the shame. It took decades to accept it; her horrific story. This past, she could do absolutely nothing to alter. A history of brutality; of rape and of torture. Of thin skin and draping bones, and an unfulfilled longing, for her history to change. She did nothing to deserve it, but of this, I am certain; she is fiercely determined, to be remade."

-Little girl speak

Little girl speak

A path to healing your inner child

By:
Sarah Kacala

"And in my little world, home was just a fancy word for hell."

-Little girl speak

Chapter 1

Before the trauma

Little girl speak

If I was completely honest with myself, there are more memories from before my trauma, than I would like to admit. It's hard for me to think back to a time, when my world was uncomplicated; when life was simple, and joy was tangible. Looking back on those memories doesn't bring me peace, but rather pain. Every early childhood memory that floods to the surface; each one is like a knife, stabbing me in the heart; bleeding me out slowly. They serve as a painful reminder, that my life used to be pretty great, and that it changed so quickly; and not for the better. But in thinking back on that simpler time in my early childhood surprisingly enough, along with the pain that accompanied those thoughts, were some key realizations that would become of use to me, in the next phase of my healing journey. And those realizations were not something that I had anticipated.

Before the trauma began, I was happy. I was so very happy and carefree. Imagine a bird soaring through the sky, singing. Imagine her landing on a tree, and hopping from branch to branch, unaware that there may be danger around her. Unaware of anything, but the smell of the crisp air and the freedom of her wings. That's what life felt like, in my earliest years of living. Carefree. Happy. Joyful. I would ride my bike in the driveway. I would play tag with my little sister, in our backyard. I remember laughing a lot. I loved the feeling of the wind in my hair, as I ran through the yard laughing and singing. And one of my favorite things to do was to lay down in the grass in the sunshine, and look up at the clouds. I remember laying there closing my eyes, as I took in a deep breath of fresh air, and let it out slowly. I remember thinking how lucky I was, to be alive. I remember thinking that I was so lucky, that I wasn't a bug, or a dog, or a fish. I felt so lucky, that I got to be a person. I felt so grateful, for my life; so happy, to be living it. Life was filled with joy, and hope, and endless possibilities. I had no idea, that that was going to change for me, very soon. There are other memories though, that came to mind as I went through this process of looking backwards. And I was surprised at what I found. As my adult self was analyzing my childhood self, there were some key truths that I realized I had ingrained in my brain, about what I was like before the trauma, that turned out not to be true. I remembered myself being completely carefree ALL the time. Happy ALL the time. Joyful ALL the time. But as I began to dig deep and really look back, I wasn't. And at first this was really upsetting for me to realize. After all, there had only been a very short chunk of my childhood that I had perceived as happy; a very short period of time, before the trauma had begun. So it made me very sad, to think that perhaps I wasn't even truly happy, during that time either. It was like an anvil was dropped on my chest; and I felt the weight of it. It crushed me. But then as I began to unpack and study those harder aspects of my personality, I was surprisingly flooded with peace, and a new sense

4

of hope. You see, another truth that was ingrained in my head, was that any anxiety or fear that I ever felt as a kid, was a direct result of the abuse I had endured. But I was now beginning to see, that I possessed some of those character traits, even before I had been abused. And that gave me hope. Because if he hadn't caused these traits to develop; if they had always been there; an inherent piece of who I was, then maybe they weren't so bad after all. And maybe I could spin them, into something good. In my mind, thinking that he had caused all of those character traits to change when he abused me; left me feeling hopeless. I felt like, if he had caused so much to change in my personality, then I was powerless to really fix it. So realizing that some of these personality traits were already there before the trauma began, gave me a sense of empowerment, that perhaps I could change things. That maybe, just maybe, as daunting a task as it would be; that perhaps I could fight back against what he had done to me, and win. Winning to me, looked like not continuing to allow what he had done; not allowing the abuse to define my life, or to control the ways in which I related to the world around me. My heart longed for freedom. And for the first time, I felt like it was possible. And that alone, was HUGE. It's hard to begin fighting a battle that you're so sure you're going to lose. Who would want to enter into a war that way; certain of their ultimate break down and destruction? I knew that I had to go into this thing; into this healing process, with a strong sense of empowerment and energy. But that seemed so impossible to me. I felt so weak; so beat down by life. I was tired. And not the kind of tired that a good night's sleep would fix. My soul was tired. My mind was tired. My heart was broken.

Looking back on my early childhood was the first step; a stepping stone of sorts. It was a test, I guess you could say. Kind of like being at a swimming pool, and walking up to the side and dipping your toes in to test the temperature, to see if it was warm enough for you to jump right in, or maybe you

needed to go over to the steps, and get into the water slowly.

Healing can feel very different, for different people. I am

NOT, a step into the water slowly kind of a person. I'm more

of the kind to just dip one toe into the water, shrug my shoul-

ders, and JUMP IN. But I knew that healing had to be differ-

ent, at least in the beginning. It didn't feel safe to me, to just

jump right in. Pushing yourself through the phases of healing

too quickly, can result in devastating side effects. The biggest

lesson I've learned in all of this, is that everyone heals at their

own pace. And you have to kind of figure out what your pace

is, as you move along. Sometimes the pace will pick up for a

while, and other times it will slow way down. Both extremes

are ok. But for most of the time, the normal pace of healing is

a slow and steady climb. It's a two steps forward, one step

back sort of thing. And I had to face these realizations right

out the gate. I needed to know what I was getting myself into,

7

at least to a degree. It just felt too scary, to leap.

Making the conscious decision that I wanted to heal, was a big one. It was a very important step. And as I continued to look back to the beginning of things; back to when I was very young and small, I realized just how loud my voice was. I laughed loud. I played loud. I spoke loud. I was outgoing and social. All of that changed, when trauma entered into my world, and shattered my heart. That was one of the many things he took away from me; my voice. But we will talk more about that later. Before the trauma as I mentioned, there were some things about me that I didn't realize were already present; personality traits that I already possessed. Core belief systems about myself that were unhealthy and unsettling. The first was anxiety. As I looked back, I realized that I had quite a lot of anxiety as a little girl. Sometimes it was just a passing feeling that would vanish after a moment or two. But other times it was debilitating, and would keep me awake at night.

Little girl speak

My younger sister came along, two years behind me. And from a very early age it was engrained in me, that I was her protector. I remember one time we were playing this game that we made up, called: Zizzybaloobah. We would put the bottom half of our legs inside a pillow case, with the pillow still in it as a padding in front of us, and we would jump all around the room, yelling Zizzybaloobah. And one time, my little sister had the idea to put the pillow case over our heads, instead of our legs. The only problem, was that unbeknownst to me when she put hers on, she put her head in the wrong side of the pillow case, leaving the padded pillow behind her face, instead of in front of it. Well you can guess what happened next: she got hurt. We were jumping around the room yelling Zizzybaloobah, and the next thing I knew, she had smacked her face on the corner of the bed, and started screaming. I tore my pillow case off my head, and grabbed hers off as quickly as I could, to survey the damage. I told her she was ok and I hugged her, as I heard my mother running up the stairs from the kitchen, where she had been making breakfast. When my mother rushed into the room and saw my sister's swollen cheek that was already beginning to turn black and blue, she turned to me and began to lay into me, hard. She smacked me a few times across the face, and across my back. She yelled at me for several minutes, and as we went downstairs all together, to get an ice pack for my baby sister's face, she told me how disappointed she was in me. That I was the older sister and that it was my job to protect her, and not let any harm come to her. She told me that I should have known better; that it wasn't a good idea to run around, with a pillow case over your head. I remember feeling very guilty that my sister had gotten hurt. I remember feeling an immense sense of shame. I also remember feeling a sense of responsibility. "It's my job." I thought. "I must protect her better from now on. Nothing like this can ever happen to her again." Now I'm certain that my mother did not mean to imply that day, that it was my job to be my little sister's keeper. But in my little mind, that's how I perceived her words. Perception can be a dangerous thing, especially for a young child. That day, I internalized the shame and guilt that I felt. I internalized the feeling of responsibility that I had, to take care of my little sister; to look out for her; to watch over her. It was ingrained in my brain that day, to be my sister's keeper. And I had no idea what it would cost me, to do so. I laughed a little bit less. I worried a little bit more. I had sleepless nights, where anxiety would probe at me, like a pitchfork. I would play out different scenarios from the day, wondering what could have happened to her, if I had not been paying extra close attention. This anxiety that was placed on me by a well-meaning mother, had chipped away tiny pieces of my joy, and my freedom. Little fragments of my childhood were stolen, as this anxiety settled deep into my bones. Looking back, of course I wish that my mother would have

11

managed to not yell at me that day. I wish she had explained things in a way that my little mind could have better understood. But I realized something about myself. Other children may have handled that situation very differently. Of course they would care that their little sister got hurt, but would they internalize their mother's words so deeply? Would they feel such shame and guilt, the way that I had experienced it? Would they have thought about it again after that day, or would they have moved on with their life, and forgotten all about it? You see, it's not just our experiences that define us; it's how WE as individuals, respond to our experiences. Each of us has different DNA, and each one of us has a different way of handling things. In a situation where most kids probably would have felt bad in the moment, but would have long since forgotten about it shortly after; I held it. I held onto it tightly, and I thought about it a lot. I allowed it to shape some truths in my mind about myself, and some truths in my mind,

12

about who I needed to become; about what was expected of me. This core belief, that it was my job to protect people close to me, had been ingrained in me BEFORE the trauma, not AFTER, as I had once thought.

Another belief that was ingrained in me at a very young age, was that I was never good enough. Once again, this was partially instilled in me by a well-meaning mother. But part of it, was of my own creation; a thought process that I seemed to be born with; an inherent character trait, that simply existed in me from the beginning. If I left a pair of clean socks on my bedroom floor, I felt guilt when my mother would scold me. If I forgot to flush the toilet, or forgot to brush my teeth; little things that most kids wouldn't even think twice about. But me? I felt guilt. I felt like a failure. This drive for perfection; this need to be perfect, began at a very early age for me. And it began BEFORE the trauma; not as a result of it. And once again, this felt like a harsh reality for me to face, yet laced with that strange sense of hope running through it. Now,

I'm going to talk about something a little bit uncomfortable

for me. Ok, something a LOT uncomfortable for me. But I

think I need to talk about it, because it shaped much of who I

was, in the beginning. These core beliefs about myself, and the

shame that I felt; a lot of it stemmed from what I am about to

say. We grew up in a religious home. Not a spiritual home. A

RELIGIOUS home. I am an advocate, of spirituality. I am all

about spirituality. What I am not about, is religion and legal-

ism. I'm sure at the time in my mother's mind; she thought she

was doing the right things. She was parenting in the ways in

which our church had instructed her to do. Maybe she took

things to the extreme a bit, but the framework of my mother's

parenting style, had the church written all over it. From a very

young age, we were disciplined in such a way that I see, as

inappropriate. When we would do something wrong; when we

would make normal mistakes that every child makes, my

14

mother would strip us down naked, lay us over her lap, and

spank us. It felt very shameful, humiliating, and unfortunately

at times, sexual. It would happen often. And the fear of having

to go through it again, instilled this NEED inside of me, to al-

ways be perfect. Often times I didn't measure up to my moth-

er's very high standards; standards which it seemed the church

had set for us. So these spankings happened a lot. And it be-

came what felt like a ritualistic thing, for my mother. I cannot

tell you how she felt, or why she allowed the church to dictate

how she disciplined her children. But what I can tell you, is

how it made me feel. It was awful. And as I began to look

back at that time in my life; the time that was supposedly BE-

FORE the trauma; I realized that perhaps such a time, never

truly existed; at least, not for me. Sure, in comparison with

what I was about to go through, what my mother did just

didn't seem like a big deal. But she continued to do this to me

and my sister, for years and years. I think the last time she did it to me; I was thirteen or fourteen years old. And when the

trauma of what was about to happen to me entered into the

picture; the combination of her discipline style, and his abuse,

was far too much for my little mind to handle. In her own un-

suspecting way, she had groomed me for what was about to

happen to me next. Looking back and thinking about all of

this, made me feel so sick to my stomach. All of these feelings

came up, that I didn't know how to process or handle. I had

remembered those earliest years of my childhood, as the hap-

piest years of my life. I remembered a joyful girl, who laughed

a lot and had a zest for life. I remembered feeling so safe, and

so loved. Now after digging deeper, and really examining

what my life was like back then, I felt like someone had ripped

open a vale, and had let me see what was behind the curtain. It

felt like I had been wearing virtual reality goggles, thinking

that it was real. Now someone had come along and had ripped

those goggles right off my face, and the actual reality was

nowhere near as pretty or as well put together, as the fake one.
And worst of all, the person who had ripped those goggles off
of my face; was me! I made the conscious decision, to look
back and dig deep. I knew that if I wanted to heal from the
trauma that had engulfed my life for so long, that I needed to
start at the very beginning of my life, and work my way
through.

That first phase of healing; the first step of looking
back to the beginning, nearly stopped me dead in my tracks;
unable to take the next step. All I wanted to do was run in the
other direction and scrap the whole thing. I felt like I had
opened up Pandora's box. And all I wanted to do now, was
close it. But it couldn't be closed. Not now; not ever. The
ways in which I was coping with my trauma, were unhealthy,
to say the least. I knew that my life couldn't continue, in the
direction it was heading. I knew that something needed to
change. And despite the horror of what I was remembering

about my early childhood, and what I was discovering about myself; I knew, that my healing needed to continue. Somehow, even in those early moments of my healing journey, I knew that every piece of my childhood mattered. Every piece was important. It was like a puzzle, that I was putting together. And if I missed even one piece, there would be no way to complete it. I had made a conscious decision, to dedicate myself to my healing. I had just looked back at my earliest years, and I had ripped out my own heart. But as I sat there holding it in my hands; this bloody beating thing, I realized something. It was still beating. I was still alive. What I had done; looking back and remembering; it didn't kill me, like I used to think it would. And for the first time, remaining emotionally absent and numb, was not my preferred choice. I realized in that moment, that if I had survived all that had happened to me, that I would survive the healing process too. And as I sat there broken, in a pile of ashes and rubble; holding this bleeding heart in my hands, for the first time in my life, I felt hope. I felt

like healing was possible, and that I could do it. One small

step at a time, and it would happen. All I had to do was

keep going.

"And you are the source of her madness;

the very core of this song of horror, that she sings.

You are a monster; the devil incarnate;

the utter ruination, of everything."

-Little girl speak

Chapter 2

The undoing

Little girl speak

When I look back at my life, I store memories and experiences in two categories: Before the trauma, and after it began. It's almost like I was two different people. I WAS the "happy" girl, before the trauma. And I HAVE BEEN the sad girl, since the day that abuse and torture entered into my world, perforating every shred of innocence, I had ever hoped to hold onto, and had claimed as my own. The trauma in essence, was my undoing. When this next step came, of having to look back at the events that had altered my childhood forever, I was undeniably terrified. I had never been able to face, what had happened to me. It always felt like too much, for my heart to handle. A weight far too heavy for my soul to bare, or my shoulders to carry. But the problem is, I had been carrying it all this time, I just didn't know it. Making the choice to not think about our trauma, does not erase it. Making a conscious effort, to remain guarded and silent about our pain, does not make it go

22

away; it channels it. It channels the pain into all the other

areas of our life. It spreads itself all over the place. And the

pervasiveness of that alone, will be your undoing, eventual-

ly. So I had a choice here. I could either face the harshest

reality; the abuse that had taken place in my life, and allow

myself to come completely unraveled and undone, in order

to rebuild, heal, and mend. Or, I could choose to remain

numb and silent, and slowly unravel from the pain, of con-

tinuing to hold it all in. Either way, I was going to unravel.

That much, I knew. And either way, it would be at my own

hands; my own doing. But at least, if I finally dealt with

what happened to me, maybe; just maybe, this heavy

weight on my shoulders might grow a little lighter. Maybe

there would be hope for me to heal, if I said the words out

loud; if I finally faced this thing, head on. Coming undone,

from choosing to deal with our pain, is a heck of a lot dif-

ferent than coming undone, from choosing NOT to deal

23

with it. Either way, I would have to deal with this eventually, or spend the rest of my life with this heavy backpack
filled with junk, weighing down my shoulders until it
would finally bury me. So I made my choice. I chose to
deal with it now. I chose to do the scariest thing I had ever
done, since I was a little girl. I chose to think; I chose to
look back at that fateful day, in all of its brutality and horror. I chose to look back, so that one day I would be able, to
look forward.

I remember the first time it happened. I remember
that entire day, from start to finish. It is a day that is permanently burned into my brain, and etched into my
memory. Every moment. Every sight. Every smell. Every
laugh. Every tear. Every shred of emotion that I felt. And
even now as I think about it; even after this rigorous healing process I put myself through for the sake of my greater
good; I still feel anger, when I think about that day. I still

feel sadness. I still feel pain. It doesn't debilitate me the way it used to, but it still hurts. It always will. I think that's important for you to know now, right out the gate. Going thought this process of inner child healing, will not erase your pain. I wish that it could. But it will help you to be able to come to a place, where it no longer defines who you are. It will bring you to a place where joy and freedom will return to your soul, and you will feel more balanced, and more alive, and better able to handle the world within you, and the world around you. That fateful day, changed every-thing. I had been playing out in the sunshine, with my little sister. Lizzy and I were running around the yard, playing fairy princesses. I was seven years old. I was wearing a Cinderella dress up gown, and a tiara on my head. I held a magic princess wand in my hand. I remember, after running around for what seemed like hours, I fell to my knees in sheer exhaustion, and laid on my back in the grass, staring

25

up at the sun. I remember how warm its beams of light felt, as they stretched across my body. I ran my fingers through the blades of grass all around me, and the smell of warm fresh air went right up my nose, as a breeze blew across the yard. And I was happy. I was so content, and at peace with my world. I remember lying there just soaking it all up; just taking it all in; all of this beauty around me. And I remember feeling so lucky, to be alive. To be a living, breathing, human being. I took in a long deep breath, and smiled as I let it out slowly. I wanted to experience every moment of my life. And as Lizzy ran over to where I was laying on the grass, and playfully tapped my belly with her magical princess wand, she let out a huge giggle, and I jumped up to my feet, and our game of fairy princess continued. I had been invited that evening, to spend the night at a friend's house. She was a friend whom I would have playdates with often. I wasn't super keen on sleeping over. I didn't sleep

26

well, in other people's houses. All the unfamiliar sounds

and smells of someone else's home didn't seem to bother

me during the day. But when nighttime came, and it was

time to go to sleep, well that was a different story. I liked to

sleep in my own house, in my own bed. I'm not really sure

why I said yes that day, to sleeping over her house. But of

course I wish now, that I hadn't. When I got there with my

little sleepover duffle bag, filled with all the necessities a

girl needs when she's not gonna be home for the night;

things like stuffed animals, and kiddie makeup, and frilly

princess pajamas, I knocked on her door. I heard her run-

ning down the stairs as fast as she could, to get to the door.

It was like she couldn't get there fast enough. She opened

the door and there I was, smiling on the other side of it. We

screamed our usual "I'm so excited to see you and spend

time with you" screams, and then I went inside. And then

for a moment, all of a sudden, I felt something. I felt

27

something I had felt a dozen times in the past, when I had agreed to spend the night at a friend's house: I felt regret. As I said, I didn't like sleeping anywhere but in my own home, in my own bed. "Why didn't I just agree to come over and watch a movie, but not sleep over?" I thought. I shrugged this feeling off, as I had felt it before. And everything always worked out fine at my other sleepover adventures. "It's just one night", I told myself. "You can sleep in someone else's house, for one night." "Hello?" She said, as I was clearly knee deep in my own thoughts. "Oh sorry." I said. She must have asked me something and I wasn't paying attention. Then she grabbed my hand and pulled me down the hallway, and off we went to play. We played board games, and make believe, and barbies. Then her mom made us dinner, and afterwards we watched a movie and had microwave popcorn. "I think it's time for you girls to go to bed now." Her mother said. "It's getting late." So

28

we went upstairs to her bedroom, and she helped me lay out

my sleeping bag on the floor, next to her bed. I had brought

my sleeping bag and my pillow from home. They smelled

like my house. That was comforting to me; the familiar

smells and textures. We did what most little girls do at a

sleepover playdate, when they're told that it's time for bed:

We laid there in the dark, quietly talking and giggling. And

eventually, we nodded off to sleep. I thought that I was

dreaming, as he came in and lifted me out of my sleeping

bag, and carried me out of his daughter's room, closing the

door gently behind him. When I realized that I wasn't

dreaming, I became confused, and fearful. "Where are we

going?" I whispered. "Shhhh." He said. "Just be quiet. I

want to show you something." He carried me down one

flight of steps, and then another, into their basement. Then

he put me down, and began to speak to me in a gentle tone

of voice, that felt safe. But the words he was saying, felt

29

strange to me. "You're so beautiful. Do you know that?" "I guess I do." I said hesitantly. "So gentle and sweet." He began to caress my face with his fingertips. "I want to show you something." He said. "Have you ever wondered, what grownups do, to show their love for each other? I could show you. It's a really fun game. Lots of pretty little girls play this game, and I can show you how. Would you like to know how to play the game? I can teach you." "Not really." I said. "Oh come on." He said. "It will be fun, I promise. You will like it. This will be the start of a secret relation-ship, between just me and you. And no one can ever know, ok?" His voice still sounded gentle and sweet. My heart was pounding so fast, that I could barely catch my breath. "No thank you." I said politely. Then the tone in his voice changed. He sounded frustrated, and angry. "You have to." He said. "You will like it. I promise. Now come here." He began to undress me, and himself. He began to kiss me on my mouth, and other places too. He began to touch me in places that felt so shameful and uncomfortable for me. And he forced me to touch him and kiss him in places that I didn't want to. "I don't like this game." I said. "You will get used to it." He said. "And if you ever tell anyone about this, I'm gonna have to hurt you and your family, and I really don't want to have to do that. Do you want your family to get hurt, all because of you?" I thought about it for a moment, as I looked up at him, just searching for any sign of kindness, or love. But his eyes looked empty now. I was frightened, and I had no idea what was going to happen next. He pulled out a pillow from the corner, and he laid me down with the pillow underneath my head. Then he turned me over, onto my stomach. He thrust himself into me. The pain was unimaginable. Searing pain, all over my body. I started to cry. He told me that I needed to be quiet. He told me that this game would hurt at first, but that I would get

31

used to it; that eventually, I would grow to like it. Every

thrust was like a bullet to the brain. It hurt so much. There

are no words that I can think of that are strong enough, to

describe the pain. I felt blood rushing down my legs. When

he was almost finished, I started to feel the pressure releas-

ing. He was taking his parts out of me. Then he made this

god awful sound that I will never be able to forget. And

then all of this white stuff came out of him, and it landed on

the carpet next to me, by my face. It smelled disgusting,

and it was slimy. I didn't know what he had just done to

me. I didn't know what this adult game was, that he was

playing with me, but I felt destroyed by it. I knew that

whatever it was, it was far beyond my years. 'Now see." He

said. "That wasn't so bad was it?" His voice sounded sweet

again, but it didn't fool me. He was a monster. What he had

just done to me, it had to be wrong. If it wasn't wrong, then

why did it hurt so much? And if it wasn't wrong, then why

would he threaten to hurt me and my family, if I ever told anyone? He laid down next to me, and cradled me in his arms. I still remember the way his cologne smelled, and the feeling of his breath on the back of my neck. It made my skin crawl. He held me captive in his arms for a few minutes, and then he began to get up. "Get dressed." He said. I put my pajamas back on, and watched him clean up my blood and his semen from the ground. Then he put it in the washing machine, poured detergent on it, and hit the start button. Somehow in that moment, even in my little seven year old mind, I knew that unlike that load of laundry; I wouldn't become clean again so easily. I knew that there was no detergent strong enough, to wash away what he had just done to me. He got himself dressed, and he picked me up and carried me quietly back up to his daughter's bedroom. He laid me back on my sleeping bag, and he didn't say a word. He just quietly

33

walked out, and closed the door behind him. I laid there, in a state of shock. Had I just had a nightmare? Was it all just a bad dream that felt real? As I began to tuck myself back into my sleeping bag, I could barely move the bottom half of my body. I was in so much pain. And I felt dried blood, all over my inner thighs and my legs. Tears began to well up in my eyes, and trickle down the sides of my face. It wasn't a dream. Whatever had just happened to me; It was very real, and it was a nightmare.

The next morning, her mom made pancakes for breakfast. Her dad walked into the kitchen, and sat down at the table and started eating and making conversation with us, as if nothing had happened. I had absolutely no appetite. I cut my pancake into small pieces, and pushed the food around my plate with my fork. "You're not hungry this morning?" Her mother asked. "Not really." I said. He glared at me from across the table. "I usually don't eat much for breakfast." I said. That was a lie. I loved break-

fast. "I'm gonna go get changed." I said. I went upstairs

and reached into my duffle bag, and grabbed my outfit that

I had picked out to bring along. I went into her bathroom,

and locked the door behind me. I took off my pajamas, and

my dirty bloodstained underwear. I rolled it all up in a ball,

and threw it on the floor. Before I got dressed, I surveyed

the damage he had done, to my body. Bruises on the insides

of my thighs, and bruises on my stomach, from being

shoved hard into the ground. My private area felt swollen,

and painful. All I could see was what he had done to me on

the outside. And the damage was severe enough. But what

he had done to me on the inside? I couldn't even begin to

imagine the extensive damage that he had done to my

mind, my heart, and my soul. I wiped the tears from my

eyes, pulled myself together, and got dressed. I went back

into her bedroom, and I shoved my dirty pajamas and

35

underwear, to the bottom of my duffle bag. "Your mom is here." My friend called from downstairs. I was never so thankful, to hear those words.

When I got home, I went right upstairs to my room. Lizzy was so excited to see me. All she wanted to do was hang out with me and play. I told her that I just needed to take a bath, and that we could play in a little while. I closed and locked my door, and I sat in the corner of my bedroom with a teddy bear, and just sobbed uncontrollably. I felt like whatever had just happened to me, was probably my fault. I felt so ashamed, and so humiliated and embarrassed. "What if his wife finds out what I've done?" I thought. "What if my friend finds out what I did with her dad?" Looking back, it makes me so sad for that little girl, that she blamed herself. I'm not exactly sure why I felt all that guilt and blame, but I did. I felt dirty. I just wanted to take a bath and make myself clean again. I ran my bath water and took off my clothes. Before I got into the tub, I stared at myself in the mirror for a while. I wanted to shatter that mirror, with a baseball bat. I was mad. I was sad. I felt different. I looked different. I sat in that bathtub for what felt like forever. I lathered my wash cloth heavily with soap and I scrubbed my body from head to toe, several times. But no matter how many times I did it, I didn't feel clean. I didn't know if I would ever feel clean again. Lizzy was knocking on my door, trying to get me to come outside and play. I got dressed, and I soaked the blood out of my dirty underwear and pajama pants, in my bathroom sink, so that my mother wouldn't see it. Then I put all my dirty clothes into the laundry, and I went outside to play with my sister. As we were running around in the yard playing tag, I saw it; I saw that spot in the grass, where I had been laying the day before, in the sunlight. I dropped to my knees, in horror. All these flashbacks of the night before, crept into my mind

37

like a horror movie being played at high speed. I laid down on my back in the grass, in that very same spot where I had been, just yesterday. But I wasn't the same little girl anymore. I wasn't the same at all. I tried to look up at the sky, and see what I saw before. I tried to be present. I tried to breathe in the fresh air, and soak up the sunlight. But all I could think about was how I wanted a do-over. I wanted to go back twenty four hours earlier in time, and somehow make things play out differently. I slammed my fists into the grass on either side of me. The sun wasn't beautiful to me anymore. It was blinding me. I couldn't see. "Tag." My sister said. "You're it." And she ran away, waiting for me to chase her. I laid there for a few more seconds, then I got up and ran after her, never to lay in that grass with joy in my heart, and freedom in my soul, ever again.

Trauma has a way of shaping and reshaping our innermost thoughts and feelings; our fundamental beliefs about ourselves, and about the world around us. It jolts our emotional inner systems, and causes irreparable systemic damage, to our bodies and our minds; no matter how hard we try to remain unaffected; unchanged. Trauma is its own life force. It takes on a heartbeat of its own, and the effects of it, run bone deep. They stretch beneath the skin's surface, and penetrate the mind, soul, and spirit within. Trauma took my already low self-esteem, and smashed it to smithereens. We are given rights as human beings, from the moment we enter into this world. The right to be treated with dignity. The right to be loved. The right to be protected and safe, and cared for. The right, to hold onto our innocence. All of those things were ripped away from me; never to return. It's a tough pill for me to swallow even now, as an adult looking back on it. Just imagine how tough a pill it was to swallow, as a seven year old child.

Trauma changes the trajectory of our lives. In

39

addition to the things that were stolen from us that can never be given back, there are other things that can come back in time, but only with very hard work, and a fierce dedication and commitment, to healing. I know that I'm making things sound bleak here, but they're not. It is very possible to heal from the horror of what's been done to you. But it certainly won't be easy. It's going to take a lot of grit, self-awareness, and determination. I wish I could tell you, that you could heal without this phase of the process; without talking about the horror itself; without getting into the details and dissecting it, to be able to process the pain and grieve it, piece by shattered piece. Every step in your healing process, is crucially important; especially this one. This one was the hardest one for me. I'm sure it will be the hardest one, for most or all of you as well. I spent my whole life, trying to avoid talking about what happened to me. I spent what felt like an entire lifetime, numbing myself out emotionally and physically, so that I wouldn't have to feel my pain. And here I was, intentionally touching it. Here I was, purposefully seeking it out; digging deep down and pulling it out of me; pulling out the most painful moments of my life, and making a conscious choice, to re-live them. But there is a purpose, in this chosen pain. I didn't choose what happened to me. I didn't choose for my innocence and my voice to be stolen. But in making the conscious choice to heal, I knew that I would come to find my voice again, one small step at a time. Intentional healing is scary. It requires us to look at our pain in graphic detail; to pick it apart and dissect its guts. But when we do, it enables us to rebuild ourselves from the ground up. We are survivors. We are living proof that a tree can still grow and bloom, out of concrete, and with winding roots. You cannot change what will be, unless you are willing to face what was. There is no doubt about it. The trauma was my

41

undoing. It altered and changed my life forever, in ways that I couldn't even begin to comprehend, as a little girl. This was the first time that I had ever thought deeply about my pain. This was the first time, that I wrote about my pain, and allowed myself to experience it and express it. I wasn't ready, to talk to anyone else about it yet. But that step would come, when the time was right. For now, just acknowledging and owning my story to myself, was enough. As I thought about my undoing, I began to write it all down. I began to journal what I was experiencing. The truth of what I was finding, was horrific. And It was very difficult to go through it alone. I knew that I couldn't go it alone much longer. But I had to be ready, to heal. I had some more looking back to do, and fearlessness to find, before I was ready to bring anyone else, into this journey with me. I had to sort through more of my story; more of the darkness, that had surrounded and engulfed my world for so long. I had to sit in the darkness alone, just a little while

longer, before I would be ready to let anyone take my hand,

and help me find my way back, to the light.

"You speak to me of roadblocks, of places where the heart stops. In hell, you can hear a pin drop. The silence is what he craves, or he won't stop. He never really did like the sound of my screaming. Only the smell of my fear and the sight of me bleeding. He put his hand on my chest, so he could hear that my heart was still beating. He killed off every sign of life that was left.

I was already dead, but still breathing."

-Little girl speak

Chapter 3

Escaping the present

A child's brain is not meant to process trauma. It's simply not built for it. A child's brain is emotionally immature, just as it should be. So when severe trauma enters into a child's world, they become frozen in time. They are suspended; unable to move forward. It stunts their emotional growth. Trauma is pervasive. It stretches itself into every permissible place, in the mind. And since children are so vulnerable, there really is no place inside their soul, that the trauma doesn't reach. Children are sponges. They soak up their early life experiences, and they create deeply rooted belief systems about themselves, and about the world around them, based on those experiences. So when a child is experiencing trauma, and their brain isn't wired to be able to process or handle it, they begin to slowly shut down inside. Children are not built to handle the complexities and the horror, of trauma. Let's face it, even the most emotionally healthy adults, have a very difficult time processing trauma; just as they should. Humans aren't meant

46

to suffer these atrocities. When I look back at myself at age seven, I begin to weep. That little girl was being brutalized. She was being raped and tortured, with no way out. She had no one safe to confide in. No one looked out for her or loved her. And no one was rescuing her, from any of it. And it breaks my heart. And so, that little girl did the only thing that she could do; she began to slowly close herself off, from the world. She started to become a hollow shell; a shadow, of the happy girl she once was. The smiles that spread themselves across her face, became forced. Her interactions with friends and family, felt fake. You see, she had to shut herself off from feeling anything; she had to become numb. What other choice did she have? Her brain couldn't process what was happening to her. She wouldn't have survived it, if she had to process it as a seven year old child. And so, she shut down. Not even on purpose at first. It was her brain's involuntary response, to what was happening to her. Her mind began to shut down and to numb itself out, in order to save her; in order to preserve her life, and the pieces of her, that still remained.

So what does it look like; escaping the present? What does it feel like? It's a very complicated question, with an even more complex set of answers. Since each of us are different, and each of us handles our trauma differently, there is no set way that the mind chooses to escape the present, in order to cope with the trauma that's taking place. For some children, it can be as simple as getting lost in a world of video games. For others, maybe it's becoming very introverted, when they used to be outgoing. Children choose to cope in all different ways, when trauma invades their universe, and threatens their safety and wellbeing. I can only speak from my own experience, and from the choices that I made; how I chose to cope, and how those choices; some voluntary and some involuntary, would come to shape my inner world, as I grew up. Quite simply, I chose food. Well, I chose the lack thereof. I chose starvation. I didn't realize at first, that this was what I was doing. I didn't realize that I was making these choices deep down, to escape what was happening to me; to turn my focus to something else, and to manage what I wasn't capable of handling or processing. I had come up with an idea that I thought was brilliant. You see, my abuse didn't stop after that one night. Even if it had, that would have been enough to destroy my innocence and shatter my inner world. It didn't stop that night; not even close. And I came up with a brilliant idea, that I was sure was going to work. I thought that if I could starve my body; if I could make myself a skinny, ugly skeleton of a girl, that he would stop raping me; that maybe then, he would finally leave me alone. I know now as an adult, that pedophilia is not about sex, but rather it is about power and control. As a young child, I didn't even think that way. All I knew was that this man continued to rape me. All I knew, was that he continued to tell me, that THIS is what pretty little girls were for. So I thought that if I wasn't pretty anymore, that maybe the abuse would stop. I also thought that if I made myself skinny and ugly like a skeleton, that my mother might see me differently; that perhaps she would see me as weak and frail, and would stop physically abusing me. And so, I made a choice. I began to starve myself. At first, it was really hard to not eat. But something happened, that I wasn't expecting. I began to like it. I liked the ache of empty, in the pit of my stomach. I felt powerful. It felt like for the first time in my life, that I was in control of my body in some way. Up until this point, other people had told me what to do with my body. They had abused me, and all I had felt, all I had known, was shame. Starving myself, gave me a feeling that I had never felt before. I thought that it was a way of taking my body back, and my voice back; a way of taking control. I had no idea that I would come to a point, where I wouldn't be able to control it anymore. For soon enough, it would come to control me.

50

Little girl speak

My friends were all eating ice cream cones, and slices

of pizza. And I was eating sliced apples, and celery. I didn't

know the name for what I was doing to myself. I just knew

that I couldn't stop doing it. It was working; but not in the way

I had originally hoped. It was working for me, in a whole dif-

ferent way. I was confused at first and surprised, by the fact

that the abuse didn't stop, despite my disappearing shape. So

my goal was no longer to make it stop, but rather to adapt to

the pain. And starvation, was working. If I was constantly

consumed with what I was eating and not eating; with calories

and numbers, and weighing myself on the scale, then I didn't

have much time left over, to think about what was happening

to me. I remember standing in front of my mirror, pinching

and pulling at my narrow curves and yet somehow, I felt fat.

The more I starved myself, the uglier and fatter I felt. I would

starve myself for days at a time. And then when I would be-

come so hungry that I couldn't handle the hunger anymore, I

would binge. I would bring bags of chips and containers of
cookies, up to my bathroom in the middle of the night. And I
would eat tons and tons of food, until I felt physically sick.
Then I would lean over the toilet, shove my fingers down my
throat, and vomit it all up, in order to avoid consuming the
calories. I remember the first time that I purged. It felt so vio-
lent, to do that to myself. I was only eight years old. With my
head leaning over the toilet, I sobbed as I forcibly heaved,
over and over again. I remember after I was finished, I just
sort of fell back and slid down on my bathroom floor, with my
back against the side of the bathtub. I was out of breath, and I
was scared to death of what I had just done. I didn't know the
name for it, but I knew that it must be dangerous, because I
felt so faint and dizzy. The room was spinning, as tears were
streaming down the sides of my face. I closed my eyes, and
imagined a completely different life; one that was very different from the life I was living. A life where my mother had not

stripped me naked, and beat me repeatedly; but rather had

loved me, and had kept me safe and protected, from the abuse

of that monster. A life where my innocence was never stolen,

and where I could be happy again, and free of all this junk and

horror, that was weighing me down so heavily inside. You see,

starvation is not about food; it's about pain. My brain wasn't

emotionally mature enough to realize, that what I was doing

may have served as a lifeboat for a little while, but was now

becoming a deadweight, that would soon drown me, at the

bottom of my own sea of pain. I was too young to realize that

this method I had chosen to cope, would not do what I hoped

it would do. I couldn't starve away, what was done to me. And

I couldn't purge it out either. I was trying to rid myself, of the

pain that I was filled to the brim with. I was trying to get rid of

gaping wounds from inside my soul, by shrinking my physical

body. I was emotionally full, and physically starving. I was

escaping the present, by using those dangerous symptoms with food, to refocus my energy and my time, and to redirect my

thoughts, to something other than my pain. And it wasn't go-

ing to work. At least, not in the long run.

I remember the first time that I cut myself on purpose.

I was nine years old. My father had been diagnosed with can-

cer, and he was dying. I was still being raped by my friend's

father, and I was still being physically and emotionally abused

by my mother. All the starvation, and the binging and purging

just wasn't cutting it anymore. I needed something else; some-

thing more, that would help me to further numb myself out,

and avoid my present situation. And so, I turned to cutting. At

only nine years old, I held that razor blade up to my arm, and I

began to make small gashes; little wounds that were dripping

blood, onto the towel I had laid out on my bathroom floor. I

was horrified, at what I was doing to myself; but I couldn't

stop. Once I started cutting, I did it often. A few times a week.

I would hide the cuts and the scars, with long-sleeved shirts in the cold weather, and with bracelets, on the warmer weather days. I had virtually no control over my world, or my body. But I could control what I ate, what I did or didn't keep down, and I could make wounds on my arms, that numbed me out a little. Yes, I was willingly choosing to hurt myself. But at least the wounds that I was making came from my own hands, and not from someone else's. And at least the wounds that I made, could heal.

As time went on, things continued to get worse all around me. My father died of cancer. I was frail and exhausted. My hair was falling out, my bones were protruding from my skin, and my arms were covered in scars, from all of the cutting. I would stand in front of my mirror, and just cry. I didn't recognize myself anymore. I was only ten years old. I was just a little girl, and I didn't want to be alive anymore. I didn't want to survive anymore. I didn't want to exist. I didn't want to keep breathing. You see, when you escape the present;

when you choose to shut yourself off from feeling anything bad, you also involuntarily close yourself off, from feeling anything good. I was still being abused. I was unable to experience joy, or laughter. I couldn't do it anymore; any of it. I couldn't handle being raped. I couldn't handle having an eating disorder, or an addiction to cutting myself. By this time, I knew what it all meant; I knew what this man was doing to me. And I knew what my mother was doing to me. And I was powerless to stop it. And I knew the names, of what I was doing to myself. I knew that I had anorexia and bulimia, and that cutting myself on purpose, was called self-harming. I felt like a FREAK. I felt damaged, and used, and worthless. As an adult, when I think back to how awful I felt, I can barely stand it. When you're a kid, you think you're so tough, and you think you're so big and so mature. I was a fragile, little ten year old child. I was just a little girl, who carried the weight of the world on her shoulders. I carried burdens and secrets that I was never meant to carry. I walked through experiences that I

was never meant to endure. I chose coping skills that were

sucking the life out of me. And I had no reason left, to go on

living this way. I wasn't living at all. I was merely surviving;

existing, at best. So here I was, at ten years old, on the verge

of making a very permanent decision. I didn't want to do this

anymore. I didn't want to live anymore. I wanted to escape the

present, permanently. I went down to my kitchen, and I got a

large knife. Then I carried it back up to my bedroom. I got my

hello kitty notebook out of my desk, and my pink hello kitty

pen. And I took the notebook and the pen, and the knife into

my bathroom, and I locked the door behind me. I scribbled out

a suicide note, on my hello kitty notebook paper. Tears were

streaming from my eyes, as I wrote about how much I loved

my family, and that I hoped they would understand someday,

that I just couldn't do this anymore. I dropped the note to the

floor, and let go of the pen. I grabbed the knife, and I held it up to my chest. My heart was racing. I took a deep breath and sobbed; riddled with fear, as I prepared to jab that knife into my flesh. And then, something happened that I couldn't explain. I felt a presence that I had never felt before. Today, I know that it was divine intervention; a mixture of God, and my guardian angels looking out for me. Back then, I wasn't sure what it was. But I felt it. And I heard it deep inside me; this still, small voice. It whispered gently to my soul: "No Sarah. Put the knife down." I released the knife from my shaking hands, and it fell to the floor. I sunk down to my knees, and laid there sobbing, all alone. I was ten years old, and there was no one there for me. I had almost just taken my life. I had spent the last two years starving myself, and mutilating my skin. I had been brutally raped over and over again and physically and emotionally abused by my mother, and no one noticed. I was just a little girl who desperately needed love; but I was invisible. I felt so alone. So unloved. So unwanted. But something, or rather someone, made me put the knife down

that day. I scrunched up that suicide note into a tiny ball,

opened up my bathroom door, and walked out; unscathed.

    I wish I could say that that was the end of my eating

disorder, and the end of my cutting; but it wasn't. Not even

close. My mother got remarried, and we moved to a different

town. I stopped going to that friend's house, and the abuse at

her father's hands, had finally come to an end. But the damage

was long since done. And my mother was still as abusive as

ever; still forcing me to strip naked, and beating me in the

most degrading and humiliating of ways. I will say this and

maintain this until the day I die: Spanking is a legal form of

child molestation and physical abuse. And no one will ever

change my mind about that. I spent my teen years, continuing

to avoid the present; continuing to willingly escape the harsh

realities of my existence, using anorexia, bulimia, and cutting

to numb myself out. After finally being diagnosed with an

eating disorder, I was in and out of treatment for the disease. Every time they took my symptoms away from me, I had to feel the weight of what was hiding beneath them. I wasn't ready to feel those things. Not yet. And so, the eating disorder continued to dominate my life. Friendships felt somewhat disconnected and distant. Life still felt meaningless. I had constant flashbacks and nightmares about being raped, and I was still living in a household with an abusive mother, and a stepfather whom I barely knew.

Writing and music became important to me. I would write poems, and quotes, and spoken word pieces. I played the piano and sang, and I took up song writing. These tools became the only positive therapeutic outlets that I had during a time when all of the inner turmoil was reaching its boiling point, inside of me. Something had to change, and soon.

I made the decision that I wanted to defeat my eating disorder. So I went into a treatment program, and I worked it as hard as I could. And for the first time in a really long time, I was doing well. I had gained weight. The eating disorder symptoms had finally started to diminish, along with the negative tapes inside my head that would play along with them, telling me that I was fat, and ugly, and worthless, and undeserving of love. I started taking college classes, and singing karaoke for fun, and playing my songs at local coffee houses. At the age of 22, I met my husband. He was 27. We spent every waking moment together. And six months later, we were married. He was the first man that I felt safe with. He was the first man that I loved. We have two children together. With all the damage I had done to my body with my former eating disorder, my doctors weren't even sure if I could have children. So my daughter is my miracle baby. She's now fourteen years old. She is brilliant and beautiful, and she teaches me and challenges me every day. My son came along when my daughter was five. He was born with down syndrome. He was diagnosed with juvenile diabetes at eighteen months, and autism at age three. My plate was beyond full. My responsibilities were heavy, but I welcomed the distraction. My marriage wasn't very healthy, and I had still never dealt with my childhood trauma at all. And all of those old feelings were starting to come back, and I wasn't ready to deal with them yet. And so, I obsessed over my son's care, in an attempt once again, to avoid the present and to refocus my energy onto something else. In this case, on someone else. I patted myself on the back. I thought that I was truly brilliant this time. I wasn't starving myself. I wasn't binging and purging. I wasn't cutting my skin. I was avoiding everything I was feeling entirely, as I hid behind the multitasking of juggling my son's care, my daughter's care, and all of the housework. I was like the energizer bunny; always moving; always going and never stopping. I couldn't stop, because if I stopped long enough, I would start to think. And if I stopped long enough to think, I would begin to feel. And I didn't want to feel. I still wasn't

there yet; I hadn't made the decision yet, to heal. On some

level, I felt like I was emotionally healthy and all patched up,

from the horrors of my childhood. But that was a lie I told my-

self. The truth is that I wasn't emotionally healthy at all. I was

distracted, and numb. And that's a big difference; that's a far

cry, from emotionally healthy. I would have told you if you

had asked me back then, that the reason why I never sat down

or rested, was because I was a very busy mother and home-

maker with two children; one of whom had multiple special

needs, and who needed me nearly every moment of the day

and night. But the truth is that while I was being a good moth-

er, I was also using my mothering as an excuse, to avoid tak-

ing care of myself; to avoid feeling all the things that I still

wasn't ready to feel, or to deal with. But reality has a way of

catching up with you, and stopping you dead in your tracks;

forcing you to come face to face with yourself, and finally

open up your wounds, so that you have an opportunity to heal them; so that your wounds can finally stop festering, and stop spilling over into every relationship in your life. On the outside, I looked like the perfect housewife and doting mother, who could do it all. But on the inside, I was emotionally bleeding out. I was silently screaming. My outward appearance was nothing more than a mirage. On the inside, I was silently deconstructing life. I was on the verge, of a breakdown. The magnitude of which, I did not see coming.

Little girl speak

"One day you'll wake up, and it won't hurt so much. You won't feel such injustice in the world, every time that you open your eyes. But it's gonna take years of processing your trauma, and of drawing from your strength deep inside. There is no healing without tears; without anger. These difficult feelings, are begging to be felt. And I am standing here begging you not to ignore them. If you do, you will lose yourself."

-Little girl speak

"Sing little birdie. Sing to me. Amongst swallowed up shores, and burning debris. Rescue me little birdie. Teach me how to spread my wings, and fly away from this place, so that I can learn once again, how to breathe. Please don't leave me alone here to die. For there is so much life, left in me."

-Little girl speak

Chapter 4

The decision to heal

Little girl speak

The decision to heal is a very personal one. It must be a conscious and intentional choice. I wish that I could tell you that I woke up one morning, with fierceness in my heart, and bravery draping from my bones, completely ecstatic about this decision; about this process, of healing. It would be like seeing the future, and being excited that you were about to get into a car crash. Not one that was going to kill you, but one that was going to hurt badly. One that was going to mar you and change you, and rip you wide open, exposing all the junk inside; leaving you with all these wounds and gaping holes that needed to be patched up, and fixed. Your pain would look visible to the world, along with your scars. No. There was nothing to be excited about, when I had finally made the decision, to intentionally embark on a journey of healing. But there were things, to be relieved about. I held onto hope, of what the finish line could look like; and it was glorious. I knew what this journey could potentially do for my soul, and I realized that no matter how hard it was gonna be; that no matter the toll it would take on my mind and my heart, that it was worth it. You know why? Because no matter what this journey would do TO me, it simply couldn't compare with all the amazing things that this journey could do FOR me. I had logically weighed it all out inside my head, and my mind was made up; I had made my decision. I was going to heal. I was fiercely determined, to rise. I was ready to take off my many masks, and to expose the horrific truths of what had been done to me, and the unhealthy ways in which I had chosen to cope with it all. I was ready, to tear my own heart out. I was ready to pull back the veil, and unearth all of the lies that were so entrenched and ingrained in me, from decades before. If you're getting this image of a warrior woman, standing on top of a hill with a sword in her hand, and a look of fierceness in her eyes, let me just stop you right there, and paint a different picture for you; the real one. Picture a woman, sitting in the corner of her bedroom in a fetal position; all curled up. On the one hand, she's a mature married woman, and mother of two.

But on the other hand, she's also battling demons that have plagued her, since she was seven years old. And she's grown too tired, to fight them off anymore. So there she sits, all curled up in the corner of her bedroom, after waking up from a nightmare, filled with flashbacks from her past. Tears streaming down her face. Hands shaking. Anxiety coursing through her veins. Engulfed by pain, in her heart. It was easy to hide from all of this during the day, when she was busy being a mother and a wife. But she couldn't escape herself, at night. When darkness fell over the sky, it came alive again inside of her too. At night, things grew quiet around her; but very loud inside her. The quiet moments created such a screaming inside of her soul; one that she couldn't bear for much longer. She was going to crack. And so, she did.

I've never been to an AA or an NA meeting, as alcohol

and drugs were never something that I struggled with. But I

had friends who had been to these meetings, and I remember

some of the things that they talk about; phrases that they

spoke to me, that were now swirling around inside my head.

These words were playing over and over again, like an old

cassette tape that kept rewinding itself to the same spot, and

was stuck on replay. There was this one phrase, that I

couldn't get out of my head, and it was just five words.

These five words, kept playing over and over again, like a

mantra; like a truth that I wasn't ready to see, but couldn't

turn away from. These five words would come to change

my life for the better, once I was finally ready to acknowledge

them, and to dissect what they meant for me personally,

on my own life path. Just five little words, with so much

weight behind them: **"My life has become unmanageable."**

Sitting in the corner of my bedroom, all curled up in the

middle of the night, these words hit me like an anvil.

I began to sob uncontrollably. "If my friends could only see me now." I thought. Then they would know the truth. They would know, that I wasn't nearly as "put together" as I seemed. I had grown so tired of all the masks I had to wear on a daily basis, just to make it through the day. I had finally reached the end of myself. My strength was depleted; my energy long gone. I had worn out the treads in my running shoes, from years of trying to stay insanely busy, in an attempt to escape myself. If you believe in a higher power, then you know that miracles exist, and that they happen all around us, and sometimes if we're lucky, they happen inside us. I believe in God, but my relationship with Him, is complicated. It's like a patchwork quilt. Its many different pieces, that don't seem to make sense on their own. But when you put them all together, they are formed into something intricately beautiful. He met me there on that dark night, in the corner of my bedroom. I felt His presence so strongly beside me. And that is the beauty in the pain; that when we have finally reached the end of our

rope, was have only reached the beginning, of His.

I had finally come undone. Life could not go on, the

way that it had been. As I said, the decision to heal is a very

personal one, and no one else can make this decision for you.

It is yours and yours alone. No one can tell you when you're

ready to embark on this journey. Only you will know. What I

can tell you though, with absolute certainty, is that you will

never feel one hundred percent ready. So if you're waiting for

some magical moment where the stars have aligned, and you

know beyond the shadow of a doubt that you want to heal, I

will urge you now, to stop waiting for such a moment to ar-

rive. No moment like that is ever going to come. I waited and

waited for my "moment," for years. And maybe in hindsight,

that was a good thing. Maybe it's a good thing that I kept

waiting, because looking back now, I was nowhere near ready,

during all those years of numbed out suppression. Another

thing that I can tell you for certain, is that there is no magical season of life, when healing is most effective. And that's a good thing. It means that it doesn't matter if you're twenty five or sixty five years old, as you're holding this book in your hands. You may be sitting here contemplating whether or not it's just too late for you to embark on this weary and tiresome journey of self-reflection, and inner healing. Well I'm here to tell you, that it is most certainly not too late. If launching my blog has taught me one thing, (it has taught me many things) it is that there is no RIGHT time or RIGHT season of life, to begin to heal. I have received messages from survivors all over the world, who are in all different stages of life, and all different stages of their healing. Some are young, and are afraid to begin the process. Some are older, and are halfway through it. And some haven't begun yet at all, and are afraid of it, but still want to do it. Only you know which category you fall into. Maybe you tried to heal once before, and your fight or flight response kicked in, and you stopped trying out

of fear. Maybe you've never tried, and you don't really know

quite where to begin. Maybe you're a person who grew up in a

family, where sharing your emotions and going to therapy,

was taboo. Maybe you grew up in a home where negative

emotions were simply never talked about out loud. There are

many many things that can come into play here; many factors

that can contribute to the fear, of beginning this process. The

common threads throughout these messages from survivors

that I continually receive are fear, shame, and guilt. But I want

to step out on a limb here for a moment, and challenge those

emotions. I want to challenge you to make a list. In your mind

right now; make a mental list. And if you're more of a visual

person, then get out a pen and a piece of paper, and write it

down. Make a list of what scares you, about healing. Then I

want you to make another list. A list of what scares you, about

NOT healing. When you are finished making these lists;

whether mentally or on paper, I can promise you, that the things on that second list will far outweigh the things on the first. You should be far more afraid, of NOT healing. Moving slowly through the muck, and forward in your life, cannot be any more painful than staying stuck where you are right now. It will not be more painful to move through, than is it to remain still. I promise you this. I swear it, on my life. Somehow, this book has found its way into your hands, and I urge you with all of my heart, to strongly consider not putting it down; to strongly consider, not giving up. Maybe you've already given up on yourself; on the possibility of healing. I'm here to tell you, that that decision can be reversed. Whether you begin this process from a state of bravery and fierceness, or whether it's just a quiet decision that you make, while curled up in the corner of your bedroom in a state of brokenness, the results are the same: YOU GET TO HEAL.

Something else I've learned, both from my own

journey, and from the countless emails I've received from other survivors, is that there is no set timeframe, on healing. For some people, it takes a year. For others, it takes much longer. For me personally, the bulk of my healing process, took two and a half years. During that time, I saw my therapist two to three times a week. I jokingly tell her now, that I did seven years' worth of therapy in two and a half years, because I went to see her so often. For me, that was an intentional choice that I made, based on how I know myself to be. I have the type of personality, where I intensely focus on whatever task I am partaking in at the moment. When I committed myself to my healing, I was ALL IN. It may be different for you, and your healing process may not look exactly like mine. As I said in the very beginning of this book, there is no exact science to inner child healing. There is no ONE way, or RIGHT way, to do this. My hope, as I've said before, is that this book can serve as a framework of sorts, for your own healing process.

I wish that I could tell you exactly how long this process will take, but I can't. Each of us is different, and each of us reacts to our trauma in different ways. So there is no way for me to know how long your healing process will take. But what I can tell you; what I can promise you, is that it will be one hundred percent worth every moment of agony. There is a saying that goes: "There is no way out, except through." That is one of the truest statements that I have ever read in my life. There are no shortcuts, but when you turn around and look back, you won't want there to have been. This process is gonna take all the grit and determination you've got, and then some. But it will come. All the strength that you need to embark on this journey will come to you. And each time it does, it will amaze and astound you. No matter how tired you are. No matter how weak you may feel in this moment, you can rest in this truth: YOU ARE BRAVE. YOU ARE STRONG, AND YOU CAN DO THIS. You CAN do this. I know you can. When you make

the conscious decision to heal, you are knowingly and willingly ripping your heart wide open, in order to be able to rebuild

yourself from the ground up; to come out on the other side of

this, stronger than you have ever been before. And that my

friend, is what bravery looks like. That is the very definition,

of brave. That is the embodiment, of courage. I don't know the

exact road you've walked. I don't know all of the painful mo-

ments and trauma that led you to this place, of needing and

wanting inner healing. But I know that our paths and our pains

have been similar. And I'm sure if we stood next to each oth-

er, you would see the same sadness behind my eyes, that's

lurking behind your own. You would see the same blisters on

my feet, from walking down so may roads, that didn't lead

toward home. But you may see a few other things in me that

you don't yet see in yourself. You may see fierceness in my

unwavering stance. You may see glimmers of hope, radiating

from my smile. You may see a peace, in my eyes. And you

79

may see hope, exuding from inside of me, like a beam of light. All of these things are the jewels that I've found, and have come to cultivate as my own, during this journey. And they are all yours for the taking. You just have to decide, that you want this; that you want to intentionally embark on this journey of healing. I can't do the healing work for you. I wish that I could. But what I can do is continue to walk beside you, in the pages of this book. What I can do, is be as honest and as vulnerable as humanly possible, about what this process looked like for me, and what it felt like. I can wear my vulnerability, like a sheer skin; transparent, so that you can see right through, to my soul. Maybe then, in sharing my own process in all of its rawness, I will be able to help you, on your own journey. That's all that I can offer you; my vulnerability and my honesty, about what this process has been like for me, and how it changed my life forever, for the better. It's all that I can give you. And I hope to God, that it's enough.

"And I have learned to make sense of these tragedies, even though I'll never understand, why there was so much suffering I had to endure. I've had to learn how to live, with all of these holes that exist inside of me. What other options did I have left? I couldn't spend my whole life, at war."

-Little girl speak

"It's ok Little One. You're safe now. I'm right here. I have

suffered in your shoes, and I completely understand. Take a

breath, and let me sit here beside you. I've got you. You're not

in this alone. Just reach out, and take my hand."

-Little girl speak

Chapter 5

A safe place to feel

Little girl speak

When you experience trauma as a child, it not only

creates an unsafe environment where you live, but it also cul-

tivates an unsafe space, inside your very own skin. When

trauma enters into the life of a child; especially ongoing trau-

ma, a permanent fear sets in. You are reminded in the most

gruesome of ways on a daily basis, that you are not safe; that

you have no control over your body, or your world, and that

there is no escape. There is no way out. This reality would be

difficult for an adult to handle. For a child? There are no

words to describe how difficult it is, to adapt to that kind of

pain. On top of all this, most children blame themselves for

what's happening to them; for the abuse that's taking place.

I've interacted with thousands of survivors since the launch of

my blog, and almost all of them; me included, did not receive

any protection or safety, within their family unit. They sur-

vived in homes where parents turned a blind eye to the abuse,

or where one or both of the parents themselves, were the

abusers. The mind of a child is not developed enough, to be able to understand or process what's taking place. So it's very common for the child to assume the blame, for what's happening to them. They internalize everything, and it morphs the rage and injustice that they feel, into self-hatred. And every blow of rejection that they receive from family members, further fuels their feelings of guilt, and of shame. So what you've got here, is a child whose will has been broken. Her reserve of strength is gone. Her innocence is obliterated, and her resilience begins to disappear. She has nowhere safe to run, and no one safe to turn to. I have spoken with a few lucky survivors, whose family members were loving and supportive, when they disclosed their stories of abuse. Those stories of supportive families who rush to the victim's side, and swoop in and rescue them, are few and far between. I cannot speak from that perspective, as that was not my experience; not by a long shot. My safety was ripped right out from beneath my skin, at a very young age. I felt like I was truly alone in the world. I was an emotionally orphaned child.

A child like that who is beaten down and broken, blames herself for everything that's happening to her. If she truly believes as I did; that it was all her fault, then she's not going to reach out for help. Why? Because she doesn't feel like she deserves to. If she truly believes that she somehow caused all of this abuse to happen to her, then she doesn't feel worthy of asking for help. And to this day, that still haunts me, when I look back at that little girl inside of me. It breaks my heart that she blamed herself for what happened to her. It was NOT her fault. It is NEVER a child's fault, that they are abused. Every child is worthy of love, and of nurturing, and of protection, and care. What happened to me was not my fault. And what happened to you, was not your fault either. I want you to really take in those words. Soak in the truth of what I'm saying, and allow it to penetrate your mind.

Little girl speak

WHAT HAPPENED TO YOU, WAS NOT YOUR FAULT.

And in case no one has told you this lately, or ever: You are

loved. I love you, and I'm so very proud of you, for surviving.

I applaud your courage, and your bravery to begin to heal. I

see you, even when you hide behind that fake smile plastered

across your face. I hear you, even when you hide your tears,

with laughter. I feel your pain, even when you disguise it and

mask it, with other things. You are not alone, and you are

loved. You are deserving of healing, and of good things. You

deserve to be happy. You deserve to be free of this trauma that

has defined your existence for as long as you can remember.

In case no one has told you these things; in case no one has

spoken these truths to you, hear me speaking them to you now.

Someone finally spoke them to me at the age of thirty three,

and now it's my turn, to speak them to you.

Ok. So I know what you're thinking. Even if this is all

true; even if none of it was your fault, and even if you are completely deserving of love and of healing; how do you go about starting this journey, and with whom? And this is a tough one. If my own parents didn't love and protect me, who else could I run to? I learned from a very early age, that I couldn't trust anyone. So even once I had made the conscious decision to begin to heal, I had no clue how to go about doing it. I knew that the process needed to be intentional, and I knew that I needed to help that little girl inside of me to process her pain, and to grow up, step by step. But how in the world could I possibly feel safe enough, to open up to another human being about this, when my own parents had proven to not be trust-worthy and safe? I needed to find a safe haven; a safe place to feel all of this junk. A safe person, with whom I could confide in, and process it all, and begin to mend my broken soul, piece by shattered piece, back into wholeness. It just felt so daunting and overwhelming to me. Here I was, bewildered and terrified. I had thought that the hardest part was over; that making the conscious decision to do this; to heal, would be the most difficult piece of this, but it wasn't. I realized that finding a safe place to feel all of this, was going to be the most difficult and most important part, of my journey. It was going to make or break me; literally. I mean think about it. You're already so emotionally drained from all the abuse you've endured. Your emotionally fragile inner ecosystem, cannot afford to suffer even one more blow, or you're going to implode. So finding a safe person, and a safe place to process all of this pain, is a critical choice. And you must choose well. Now I'm not going to say that you can't choose the wrong person and figure that out, and move on to find the right one, or that you can't find a way to heal in spite of not having a therapist who is best suited for you. That's not what I'm saying at all. But it does make opening up harder, if you don't feel comfortable or safe. I confided in a few unsafe people, toward the beginning of my healing process. And yes I'm not going to lie to you, the rejection was brutal and damaging to my fragile psyche. But I picked myself up, dusted myself off, and kept searching for that safe person. I think the long term damage happens, when this decision is made poorly, and we don't see the signs that we've chosen an unsafe person, and continue to confide in them; further damaging ourselves instead of walking away, in search of a safe individual. So it's really important, that you find a safe person and a safe place, to feel and process your pain, and to begin to heal. Further damage to your self-esteem, could be catastrophic, if you don't choose wisely. So let's talk for a moment, about what a safe person looks like; what characteristics they possess, because maybe you don't even know. I didn't know at first. When children grow up in an unsafe environment, they have a hard time knowing who's safe, and who isn't. For me, I felt invisible as a child. I used to tell myself that it was my superpower; my invisibility. But being invisible was very hurtful and very damaging to me. I felt like no one ever listened to me, or loved me. So when I first decided

to heal, I didn't know who was safe and who wasn't, because

no one had ever really talked to me on a deep level before. I

had done residential treatment for my eating disorder as a

teenager, but that was the only place where people spoke to

me about what I was feeling on the inside. And I know that

each one of us may need something different. For example, for

me I knew that I needed a person or a few people, who were

compassionate and caring, as I never had that around me,

growing up. I needed love and nurturing, and I needed to

know that I was in an environment where I wasn't going to be

judged, or blamed for what happened to me. I needed to know,

that I was going to be validated, and supported. A safe person

is someone who is not going to judge you. A safe person is not

someone who believes that prayer alone can heal trauma. We

will get more into that later. A safe person, is not someone

who's going to "tough love you to death" until you pretend to be healed. From my perspective, these are the words that describe the character of a safe person: Kind, caring, warm, compassionate, empathetic, grounded, self-aware. No human being is perfect, but I think it's safe to say that we've been damaged enough as it is as a survivor, and we don't need to add any more traumas to that lengthy list we've already experienced. It became clear to me, that besides finding one or two safe friends to confide in, that therapy was a must and that it would serve as the main supportive environment, for my healing and my growth. So now I knew where to start: Therapy. Therapy was going to serve as the environment, where most of my healing would take place, and it would serve as the framework, for helping me to develop the tools that I needed along the way, to mend my broken soul. When I searched for a therapist, I looked for those same qualities that I looked for, in the friends whom I could potentially feel safe enough with, to confide in. I looked at their professional profiles, and tried to get a sense of who they were, and what their personality was like. It wasn't easy. I was trying to choose a person who would walk with me, and help me navigate through some really difficult stuff. I wasn't looking for perfection. I was looking for safety, compassion, encouragement, and love. And I found it. I found the right therapist for me. And when I found her, it changed everything.

I remember the first time I met Ali. Her office was warm, and welcoming. I sat down on a sofa, across from her chair. She was very soft spoken, and kind. She asked me why I had decided to come to therapy; what had brought me to her office. Boy was that a loaded question, with some complicated answers. I looked all around her office, and studied the decor. I looked at the pictures on the walls. They were very peaceful. I looked at knickknacks she had, sitting on an end table next to the couch, and on the window sills. Even her window treatments were peaceful and tranquil. And I paid attention, to her body language. She was relaxed, and calm. She began to ask me different questions, about my current situation; about what my home life was like. I spoke very matter of factly, and without emotion. I tried to keep myself completely composed. I didn't want her to realize what a mess I felt like, on the inside. I logically understood, that therapy was like the ONE place in the world, where you're supposed to let it all hang out; where you're supposed to not hold back, and just say how you feel. I get that therapy is a place where you can cry, and vent, and be completely safe to be your authentic broken self. But it takes a little time to feel safe enough; even with a safe person, to open up like that and bare your soul. She began to ask me questions about my childhood. I felt a lump in my throat, as tears began to well up in my eyes, but I held them in, and I choked that lump right back down. This was our first session, and there was no way in hell this woman was gonna see me cry. I never cried in front of anyone. Since I had grown up in a home where we were shamed if we cried or felt our feelings, I had learned to cry by myself; when I was alone and then eventually, not at all. That dark night months earlier, curled up in the corner of my bedroom; that was the first time that I had cried in a very long time. And it had been years, since I had cried in front of another human being. I couldn't believe that I was about to cry in front of her. It actually scared me, but in a good way. "She can help me." I thought. I knew in that moment, as I swallowed the lump in my throat and held back my tears, that she was the right therapist for me. So I took a deep breath, pinched myself to keep from crying, and I rattled off my story, like I was reading a manual from the glovebox of a motor-vehicle. Very matter of fact; no emotion in my voice. I didn't get into any graphic details, but I told her the outline of my story; the basic bullet points of my life that had led up to this moment in time. She was writing things down, as I was talking. And when I was finished, she

95

looked up at me, with tears in her eyes. "Why aren't you cry-

ing?" She asked. "I don't know." I said. I hadn't cried in front

of anyone in such a long time. I felt ashamed to cry. I felt

scared that if I started crying, I may never stop. She proceeded

to tell me that I had been through so much horror and trauma

in my life, and that she didn't know where to begin. I was

scared that she was gonna tell me that my story was just too

hard; that it was just too much for her to handle; that I, was

just too much, for her to handle. But she didn't. She just sat

there staring at me, with this sad look on her face. It was like

she could see me; the real me. She could see the me that I

didn't show to the outside world. As I look back on that day I

realize now, that even though I knew she was the right thera-

pist, I just didn't feel quite safe enough yet, to let her in. Cry-

ing in front of her would be a huge step for me, and it was not

a step that I was not ready to take yet, on that first day. But I

knew that soon enough, it would happen; that I would be

ready, to let her in. For I had found my safe person. I had found my safe place, to feel. There isn't an exact science, to finding the right therapist for yourself, but I can tell you this: When you find the right one, you'll know. And when you find them, that's when this journey starts to take on a life and a pulse of its own. That's when the true growth and healing, begins.

"And the storm clouds raged, all around her.

And the sound of the thunder, roared through her veins.

The crack of the lightning,

pulsed through her skin like a second heartbeat,

beckoning her demons, to awaken;

calling them to come, so that she could trample

them under her feet, the moment she started to run."

-Little girl speak

Chapter 6

Entering into the darkness:
The re-traumatization phase

Little girl speak

I refer to this next stage of my healing process, as: "going dark." And I'm going to explain why I feel that way about it, and why it's so vitally important, not to ignore the dark spaces inside of us; those purposefully hard to reach places, where everything feels raw, and better left unexposed. Those secret, bottomless seeming caverns inside our souls, where we're so desperately afraid to roam and walk around in, out of fear that we will never come back up to the surface. We fear that I we go in, we may never be able to come out again. And I've got some disheartening news for you. There will be times, when you will feel as if you're never going to be able to survive your healing. There will be times when you will be almost certain, that you cannot take another step forward. There will be moments when you are almost sure, that you will never again, see the light of day. But the good news, is that as much as those moments will hurt; as scary as they will be, they don't have to define you, and you don't have to let them knock

100

you off course. Those moments won't break you, if you

choose to let them REMAKE you. It is not in the light,

where you will find the essence of your soul; it is in the dark-

ness. Trudging through the most horrific moments of your

childhood, is where you will finally begin to crack open, a lit-

tle bit at a time. And every wound that's made, will become an

empty space, and then the empty space will fade, into a scar.

And when it first starts to happen, you will hate those scars on

your soul. You will feel them. You will swear to God that they

can speak, because you will hear them. You will hear the

whisper of demons past; of those who taunted, and tormented

you as a child. But you will begin to discover something beau-

tiful, in the breaking; that there is beauty in your scars; that

when you sit with them long enough without trying to escape

from them, they begin to take on a new meaning and a new

shape, much like the turning of a kaleidoscope. In your coura-

geousness and in your willingness, to unzip and unlock the

101

deepest caverns of your soul, you are consciously choosing to be brave. Some days, you won't feel brave. Some days, you won't look like Webster's dictionary definition of the word brave. But believe me warrior soul, YOU. ARE. BRAVE. Healing these deep wounds inside of us is hard work. It is incredibly difficult work. And even on our hardest of days, we are counted as warriors, and we are brave. So just remember this truth, when you're in the trenches. Hold onto this truth: that you CAN do this; that you CAN KEEP GOING, and that you are BRAVE enough, to keep putting one foot in front of the other; to keep taking the next step forward, even when you're afraid to move. When you're shoulder deep in the weight of your trauma, it's hard to see anything but the storm that's raging around you, and inside of you. But those are the moments when you have to hold on, with every shred of fierceness, that's left inside of your aching body. Those are the moments, when you have to consciously choose your healing all over again. Those are the dark moments, when you have to tell yourself that giving up, is simply not an option. Those are the defining moments, when you have to remind yourself, that you were built for this; that you were made, for freedom; that you were designed, to break through.

So let's talk about what it means to "go dark," and why it's so important. "Going dark," is an intentional decision, to touch the deepest pain inside of you. It is making a conscious and willing choice to mentally and emotionally go back in time, and in essence, relive the trauma you once endured. That is why I call this, the re-traumatization phase. Throughout your journey of healing, there will be things that will trigger your trauma; things that will cause you to have a flashback, or will make you feel sad for a period of time. I wish I could tell you that the triggers will eventually go way completely, but I have not found this to be true. Unfortunately, they don't. But they will lessen more and more, as time goes by. And the further along you get in your healing process, the more you will learn how to manage your triggers in such a way, that they won't have such a profound effect on your state of mind, or your mood anymore. I know that this all sounds so bleak, but I promise you that in the end, it is well worth it. Your healing is invaluable. You cannot put a price tag on it. This journey of healing may be the second hardest thing you've ever done in your life, but it's not the first. You already survived the trauma itself. You have already endured immense pain, and suffering. The initial trauma will always hold that first place position. It will always rank number one, in the "hardest things you've ever done" category. So if you think you're not strong enough to survive this healing process, think again brave warrior. Think again. If you were strong enough to survive the trauma, then you are most definitely strong enough, to survive the healing.

"Going dark," may not be something that you are ready

to do right away. For some people, it may take months of ther-

apy sessions, before they feel completely ready to dig deep

into their traumatic past. For others, it may take only one or

two sessions, before they feel ready. For me, it took about a

month or so. As I mentioned before, I already knew from that

very first session with my therapist, that she was a the right

person to walk alongside me, through my healing journey. But

just because I knew she was the right person, that didn't mean

that I was immediately ready to delve into places inside my

heart, that I had kept hidden from the outside world for so

long. Each of us is different. There is no set time frame, for

any of this. It's ok if you feel ready to talk about your trauma

after only one session, and it's also ok if you don't feel ready

to talk about it, until you're thirty sessions in. This is YOUR

healing journey and yours alone. No one can do this work for

you, and so no one has the right, to tell you when you're ready

to do it. The mark of a good therapist, is when

they gently nudge and push you emotionally, but don't shove

you into healing. And what I mean by that is this: While ther-

apy is supposed to be a safe place and a safe space, to honor

your feelings and to process your pain, it's kind of like yoga.

Not every position in yoga is comfortable. In fact, many yoga

positions have moments of discomfort in them. But you have

to find the comfortable spaces, within the discomfort, and al-

low yourself to breathe through it; to breathe through the pain.

Therapy is similar. There will be times when your therapist

will sense that you need a nudge; just a tiny push in the direc-

tion of opening up further, and sharing more of the pain that

brought you to this place in your heart, where you currently

reside. If a therapist is gently pushing you to talk about things

that make you uncomfortable, that's normal; that is to be ex-

pected. Being uncomfortable is a part of therapy. It is the part,

where growth and change begin to take place. But a good

therapist, will never tell you that you HAVE to talk about

something. They will gently push you, but they will never shove you in the direction of your healing, because they know that the choice must be yours, and yours alone. So don't beat yourself up, if you don't feel ready right away, to dig deep. Take your time. Once you begin to "go dark," it's gonna be a while, before you resurface again. You're never going to be one hundred percent ready for it, but you want to make sure that your therapist is the right one; that you feel safe with them, and that they are a person who is compassionate and caring. Because once you open up that door to the past, you won't be able to close it so easily again. And you're gonna need a good therapist by your side, as you embark on this journey toward wholeness; this path, toward finding your inner joy and peace, once again.

No one wants to talk about pain. It's hard for all of us, but it's necessary. Your heart won't mend, if you don't. You cannot heal, what you do not acknowledge. You have to feel

107

it to heal it. I had decided that I was ready to "go dark," but I didn't know how to do it. I tried a few times, to open up to my therapist. I tried to just start a conversation about my trauma, or to answer questions that she was asking me about my trauma. But it's like someone was wrapping their hands around my throat, cutting off my air supply. The words just wouldn't come out. I don't know if it was fear, or shame, or a mixture of both, but everything was bottled up inside of me, and I was about to implode. I knew that it needed to come out. All of it; everything I had stuffed down for decades of my life. I couldn't take it any longer, but I couldn't bring myself to say the words. They just wouldn't come. So I had to find a way. I couldn't stay like this. So much time and thought, went into this conscious decision to break myself wide open. And now here I was, unable to speak! It would be like taking a baseball and throwing it at the ground, expecting it to break like an egg. I realized in that moment, sitting there in Ali's office on her couch, in a safe space, with a safe person, that after dec-

ades of forcibly keeping all of this junk bottled up inside of

me, that even I, couldn't force it to come out. My heart, was

once like an egg; fragile and delicate. Emotions were real and

teaming along the edge of the surface. But years of trauma and

living with hidden shame as a result of it all, had eroded away

at my soul. I had built up walls so tough, and so high around

me, that I had transformed myself into something hardened

and impenetrable. I realized in that moment, that my walls

were so high, that even I couldn't scale them. Not only could

she not get in, but I couldn't get out. I was trapped inside;

alone and terrified. I sat there on her couch in silence, as all of

this knowledge and truth was just swirling through my head

like a tornado. She asked me what I was feeling. I looked up at

her with a blank stare, but what I was feeling inside, was

hopelessness. I had just realized that all of this mental work I

had done, to come to this place where I was finally ready to open up to another human being about the horrific pain I had

endured; that all of that work, was for nothing. It was just too

hard. My walls were just too high. I stared up at them; those

thirty foot high brick walls, inside my heart. I didn't know

how to climb them. I did my best to get through that session

with Ali, and when I left her office that day, I choked back

tears, the entire way home. Why couldn't I do this? Why

couldn't I cry? What was wrong with me? I had numbed my-

self from the pain for so long, that I couldn't feel it anymore.

My walls were too high to climb, and I couldn't feel anything.

I couldn't feel pain, or joy. I just felt empty, and I didn't know

what to do. If I wasn't going to be able to heal, then what was

the point in living anymore? I wasn't even really living at all. I

was merely existing, and my soul was a so incredibly tired.

The kind of tired, that no amount of sleep could fix. That

evening, an image and an idea came to me. I closed my eyes,

and I saw myself. I was me, but not the adult me. I was a little

110

girl again, and I was standing in front of this huge brick wall.

It was so high, and it stretched as far to the left and right, as I

could see. And there was no way around it. The only way, was

up and over; or so I thought. There was this huge hammer,

laying on the ground. I thought that it would be way too heavy

for me to pick up, but it wasn't. And there I was; a little girl,

standing in front of this huge brick wall, holding a hammer. I

screamed, as I swung as hard as I could. On the first swing, I

only saw a small dent in the brick. But then as I kept on

swinging and hitting it, I realized that I was breaking it; the

wall was starting to crack. I stood there tired; breathing heavi-

ly. And then just like that, I knew exactly what I needed to do.

"I don't have to climb the wall." I thought. It may be too tall

to scale, but it isn't too tough, to break down into pieces. I

wasn't going to be able, to go up and over it. I was going to

have to go THROUGH. I was going to have to break it down.

And as I laid my head on my pillow that night, I was fiercely determined to find a way.

For the next few days, I moped around with lost enthusi-asm. I had felt so empowered the night before, to find a way to break down this brick fortress, that I had spent the last twenty six years of my life constructing, between me and the outside world. But in the harsh light of day, I had absolutely no idea how to do it; how to knock it down. "I can't do it brick by brick." I thought. "That would take FOREVER." No. No no no. I was NOT going to dismantle that wall, one brick at a time. I was determined, to take a wrecking ball to that thing, and to demolish it, with one hit. And by the end of that week, I knew exactly how I was going to do it. For as far back as I can remember, I have been a writer. I've always written. Quotes, poems, songs. Words had always had a way with me; and I with them. They had always found a way to seep through my veins, and claw their way up to the surface, and onto the page. It was a brilliant idea. I was going to sit down, and write about my trauma, then I wouldn't have to sit there anxious during therapy, trying to force the words to come out. All I was going to have to do was read them.

It was two days before my next therapy session with Ali, when I sat down to write about my trauma. I had decided to use my computer to type, instead of writing it out on paper. I did it that way, for a few reasons. The first being, that I am a lefty. And all left handed people know, that when you're righting too quick, words tend to get smudged on paper. And I couldn't afford for one word, to not be legible. And the second reason, is that I can type very fast. I wanted this piece that I was going to write, to be a stream of consciousness. I didn't really want to think about it as I was writing it. I just wanted to get it out, as quickly and as efficiently as humanly possible. So I sat down with my laptop fully charged, and ready to go. I took a long deep breath, and began to type.

There they were, in all their ugliness; hundreds of words

strewn together, making these complete sentences, that reminded me how utterly incomplete I felt, on the inside. My body ached, from what I had just done. It felt like someone had reached inside my chest, and had ripped my heart right out, and then crushed it, in front of my eyes. I managed to keep myself composed, and emotionally absent from the experience, as much as I could. I choked down lump after lump inside my throat, and didn't allow myself to cry. I told myself that typing it out was enough emotion expressed for one day. I printed it out, and I folded it and put it in my purse. I didn't let myself look at it or think about it until two days later, when I stepped into Ali's office again.

"You seem nervous today" she said, as I sat on the edge of her couch, pensive. Legs shaking; unable to sit still. Riddled, with anxiety and fear. I knew what I was going to have to do before that hour was over; before our session would come to a close. I was going to have to read her what I had written, about my life; about the trauma I had experienced. I

sat there just wrestling with myself; deliberating about wheth-

er or not I should even read it to her at all. But in my heart, I

knew that it didn't matter how difficult it was going to be. I

had to do it. If I wasn't going to take a wrecking ball to that

giant brick wall, then what was I doing there? What was the

point, of going to therapy? "There's something I have to read

you today" I said, staring down at the floor. "Ok." She said.

"It's about my childhood. It's about um, the things that hap-

pened to me. How they happened. When they happened.

When it started." I thought about having her read it, so that I

wouldn't have to say the words out loud, but something inside

of me, screamed no. I knew deep down, that I needed to be the

one to speak those words. I needed to speak them out loud, to

another human being. This was going to be the first time in my

life, that my story was going to be shared in graphic detail,

and it needed to be shared, with my own voice speaking it. I needed to own my story, no matter how painful it was going to

be; no matter how much fear and shame I was feeling about it,

in that moment. I reached into my purse, and pulled out my

poem; this godawful stream of consciousness I had written. I

opened it up, and I wasn't sure if I could do it. I didn't know if

I could let her in. My hands were shaking, and my palms were

sweaty. "I didn't think I could really talk about this, so I wrote

it all down in a sort of poem." I said. "Ok." She said. "Do you

want to try to read it to me?" I nodded. But I didn't want to

read it. I could see the door, in my peripheral vision. All I

wanted to do was leave those pages there for her to read by

herself without me in that room. I just wanted to get up, and

run right out that door to my car, and leave. I wanted to run for

the hills. "Don't run." I thought. "Just disconnect. Don't be

present. Just disconnect." But something happened, when I

started reading my poem to Ali. I couldn't disconnect. I

couldn't separate myself, from what I was reading. I was

fully present in that moment. I was reading about my life; about what had happened to me, and I couldn't run from it anymore. I couldn't outrun my trauma. It had caught up with me. Something about her made me feel so safe, that my mind was refusing to disconnect, or disassociate. And all of a sudden, it was happening. I was sharing in graphic detail what had happened to me. I was sharing the depth of my pain with another human being. Tears began to stream from my eyes and down my face, as I spoke the words out loud; as I owned my story in all of its horror, for the very first time in my life. And as I read it out loud, I realized just how bad it was; how much trauma I had survived, and just how much pain I had truly been in, all this time. I won't go into graphic details about that poem I had written, but the gist of it, is that my friend's father had raped me for four years of my life. When I was a little girl, from the ages of 7-11, I had survived immense torment and torture. Tears were streaming down my cheeks. I couldn't stop them from coming. When I was finished reading, I was still looking down at the pieces of paper in my hands, in shock and utter disbelief. I couldn't believe that I had finally shared my story with another human being. All I wanted to do was hide. I felt so much shame. It all weighed down so heavily upon me. She reached for a tissue, from the box on the table. I looked up from the tattered pages in my hands. Ali was sobbing. No one had ever cried with me before. I often tell her now, that she saved that little girl's life that day; that she saved MY life that day. Ali was the first person to ever show me empathy and compassion. She was the first person who cried with me. She was the first person who ever nurtured my inner child; the first person, who made me feel safe enough inside my own skin, to be able to process my pain. That therapy session, was a game changer for me. It will always have a permanent place, in my heart. Nothing was the same after that. That powerful therapy session, changed the entire trajectory of my life.

Little girl speak

Owning my story out loud for the very first time had a profound effect on me. One that was deeper than I could have ever imagined. And having someone really listen to me for the first time; having someone open up their heart, and choose to feel the crushing weight of my pain alongside me; someone who chose to sit with me, and cry with me in my darkest moments; there are no words to describe that kind of compassion. It literally felt like she took a piece of my pain onto herself, and cried the tears out for me. It was the first time that my pain had ever been recognized; the first time that my feelings, had ever been validated. When you share your story, you can do it the way I did; you can write it down in the form of a poem. Or you can write it out in plain sentences. Sometimes reading it from a piece of paper is easier. Or if you have the courage to just speak it from your heart, without writing it down; if unlike me, you don't feel like there are invisible hands around your throat choking you, and then speak it out loud from your heart, on the spot. Maybe you are an artist. Maybe you can paint, or draw a picture of what happened to you, with words surrounding it, to describe how the trauma made you feel. You must find a way that works for you, to take a wrecking ball to that giant wall, between you and the outside world. And when you do, make sure that you are doing so with a safe person. You need to know that you are safe; that when you have finally worked up enough courage to share your story with another human being, that you will be met with compassion, care, and empathy. You can do this. Yes, it will feel re-traumatizing at first. Yes, you will find yourself reliving those horrible moments that you've spent decades of your life trying to bury and forget about. You will find your-self sitting in a huge heap of ashes and rubble, when that wall is gone; when you've shared your story. But there is beauty in finally reaching the bottom. For it is from that space, that there is no place left to go but up. It's wrecking ball time. It's time for the wall to come down. It's been up for long enough now,

don't you think?

"I am spinning storms inside my head.

They leak out, like tiny hurricanes.

I apologize for letting them loose all around me,

but some days I can't hold all that pain."

-Little girl speak

Chapter 7

Conversations with a 7 year old

Little girl speak

This next phase of my healing journey came with some really devastating realities; ones that just seemed too awful to face. But I also knew that continuing to run from them, was simply not an option; not if I wanted to feel better. Not if I wanted to mend and heal. Early on in the therapeutic process, I had come to realize something; a very devastating something. I had realized that a part of me had never grown up. Here I was, a thirty three year old married woman and mother of two children and in most ways, I was a very mature and level headed person. But there was in fact a part of me; a part of my mind and a part of my soul that was still trapped as a seven year old little girl; suspended in time; unable to grow up. I realized that a part of my heart and a part of my brain had been frozen in time, for decades of my life. This truth hit me about as subtly as a hurricane. So what was I going to do now? How in the world was I going to heal, from all of this damage that had been done to my psyche? It all just felt so overwhelming again. It felt so strange to me. You see in some ways, being abused had forced me to grow up so quickly. In some ways, I was forced to be an adult, at just seven years old. But in other ways, the abuse had suspended my emotional growth; keeping me trapped in time, holding wounds that needed to heal, in order for me to be able to move forward and to grow. This truth made me so angry. As a child, I was forced to be an adult. And now as an adult, I was forced to go backwards and to allow myself to be the angry kid that I should have been in the first place, who couldn't handle what was happening to her. It all just seemed so unfair. My childhood had been stolen from me, and now it seemed as if I was going to be robbed of my adulthood as well. I knew that this process of healing was going to be long, complicated, and miserable. But I had barely left the starting gate, and I was already ready to throw in the towel, and give up. And since I had already decided that giving up was not an option, I knew that I had to reframe the way that I viewed this whole process, in my mind. I needed to reframe the way that I saw it, so that I could experience it through the eyes of hope, rather than through a lens of trauma and hopelessness. And so, that's exactly what I did. I changed my perspective. I tried to look at this process, through a different lens. "It was a process of regrowth," I told myself. I was going to have to grow myself up all over again, inside my adult body; inside my adult skin. I was going to have to help that broken little girl; the one who was trapped inside of me. I was going to have to heal her shattered heart, so that she could begin to feel whole again. I realized that the only way for me to heal, was to heal her. I needed to grow her up inside of me, step by step. I needed to heal her pain, layer by excruciating layer. It was the only way that I would ever find the freedom and wholeness that I was searching for. She was the key. Her freedom was the key to my own.

Ok. So there it was, in all of its horror and rawness;

126

this process of healing laid out before me. I now had a frame-

work. I knew exactly what I needed to do. I needed to grow up

that little girl inside of me, so that I could reclaim my life, and

be happy again. Simple enough, right? NO. HELL NO. A RE-

SOUNDING HELL NO. I couldn't sugar coat this process, to

myself. I could barely wrap my mind around it, quite honestly.

I couldn't convince myself that this would even be remotely

attainable, let alone easy; because I didn't think that it would

be. I knew what I needed to do, but I just didn't know if it was

possible. And even if it was possible, how in the world would

I survive it? All of these questions swirled around in my brain,

as I pushed my shopping cart up and down the grocery store

isles. I remember glancing at a woman across the aisle as she

shopped, and I thought to myself: "Does she have inner child

healing to do?" Then I looked at another woman and thought:

"I wonder if she's broken too, and if she is, I wonder if she

even knows that she's broken." I didn't know I was broken;

127

not this broken anyway. I had a major panic attack, in the middle of the grocery store. I left my cart where it was, in the middle of isle nine, and I made a run for it. I darted out to my car as quickly as my feet could carry me, and I sat there dizzy, just trying to catch my breath; just trying to drown out all the commotion, inside of my head. My chest was tight. My breathing was shallow. My thoughts were racing, and my brain would NOT slow down. It would not shut up. It wouldn't leave me alone. I was analyzing my own thoughts and feelings to death. I was dissecting and disintegrating my self-worth in the process; in one fowl swoop. Was I having a nervous breakdown? Is this, what having one felt like? I couldn't stop the incessant questions from coming. I literally screamed at myself in my car that day. I yelled at the top of my lungs: "Sarah, SHUT UP!" And then, it hit me. None of this questioning, was me; It was her. None of these thoughts were mine; they were hers. I wasn't talking to myself, when I told myself to shut up. I was talking, to her. What was happening to me? It felt like therapy was somehow making me crazy. Talking about my childhood had awakened her; this broken child, who lived inside my bones. And now, I couldn't shut her up. I guess after years of being forced to be silent, she had a lot to say. She had a lot of questions for me and I didn't know any of the answers; at least not yet. I didn't know if I could handle this; this idea of growing her up inside of me. I just wanted to shove her back into the silent void from which she came; never to hear from her again; never to have her voice return. But that's what THEY did to her. The man who had abused her and even her own mother. They had silenced her voice. They had forced her to bury her pain. And no matter how hard it was going to be to heal her, I had to figure out how to make it happen. After everything she had been through, she deserved that much; she deserved to heal. I couldn't stifle her tears. I couldn't avoid her questions. I couldn't silence her pain. I wouldn't do that to her. I just

couldn't do it. I had to find a way, to merge she and I together.

I had to find a way to quiet her voice within me, so that I

could breathe. I was going to have to mother her. I was going

to have to calm her fears, and nurture her. I took some more

slow deep breaths, sitting in the driver's seat of my car in the

grocery store parking lot, on that crisp autumn day. And as I

watched the leaves falling from the trees all around me, I

made a promise to her, that everything would be ok.

As the days pressed on, her voice grew louder and

louder inside of me. She was needy. She was clingy. She was

broken, and afraid. I remember sitting in Ali's office, exhaust-

ed. I was tired. I was bone tired. This seven year old little girl

was taking over my mind. I didn't have time for this. I didn't

have time for her. I had two children of my own to take care

of, and a husband, and a house, and laundry, and cooking, and

cleaning, and the list goes on and on. And my inner life, was becoming more complicated than my real life. "Ali, I hate

her." I said. Arms crossed, legs shaking with anxiety. "She's

an annoying little shit, and I hate her." Ali just calmly nodded,

and let me get it out. "She won't shut up. She never shuts up.

She's triggered by everything. She asks so many damn ques-

tions all day long. She's always whining and crying and carry-

ing on like an enraged toddler, and I don't know what to do

with her. I don't know how to fix her. I just know that I can't

stand her, and I want her to leave me alone." Ali just nodded.

"Ok." She said. I wanted to scream! It was so infuriating!

She's the one who helped me open the door for this annoying

little brat to come out. Was she going to help me get rid of the

little pest or not?! "Don't you think you're being a little hard

on her?" She asked. I looked up with a look that probably sent

chills up and down her spine. "What?" I said. "I get that

you're angry at her," she said. "It's sad, but it's normal. Get it

all out. Let it out. Once you've allowed yourself to be free to hate her, you'll be able to see the truth and embrace her." Ali

was right. I was being hard on her. Why did I hate her so

much? Why did I expect so much from her. "She should have

told someone." I said. "Maybe." Ali said. "But she was only

seven and she was afraid. You were only seven." I felt tears

welling up in my eyes, and I couldn't stop them from falling.

"I don't think I can fix her. I think she's gonna be stuck like

this forever, which means I'm gonna be stuck like this forev-

er." Ali moved to the edge of her seat. "Sarah, look at me. I

want you to look at me." She said. "I swear it won't always

feel like this. It won't, but it's gonna feel like this for a while."

When I left her office that day, the things that she said to me

were resonating louder than the voice of my inner child. Ali's

voice could be heard, above my inner noise. "Once you free

yourself to hate her, you will see the truth and embrace her." It

played over and over again, like a mantra inside my head. I

decided to write to her; to that little girl inside me. I was going to sit down and write her a letter. I was going to get all of my thoughts and feelings out on paper and sort through them. I needed to sift through the lies I had told myself about her and discover the painful truths. After all, being angry at her was far easier than being sad about what she had endured. Angry was safe. Sad? Not so much. For some reason, sadness made me afraid. I had no idea what I would say, when I wrote to her. I just knew that I needed to get it all out; all of these jumbled up thoughts, inside my brain. I needed to sit down and write them all out. I needed to etch them, onto the page.

By the time I had finished writing her the letter, I was sobbing. I realized, that we truly do need to honor all of the feelings that we have, during this process. Even the ones, that don't make sense to us at first; especially those, because they usually end up being the feelings that catapult us into further healing. The most painful truths we experience during this process, will be the very things that cause the light to shine even brighter, at the end of this dark tunnel. Ali was right. I

was being way too hard on that little girl. I was expecting way

too much from her. I was angry at her for reasons that didn't

make sense, even to me. I was angry over things that she had

no control over and I knew that my interaction and my dia-

logue with this little girl, needed to drastically change. She

didn't need another adult in her life who didn't care about her

feelings. She didn't need another adult in her life who would

tell her to be quiet, and sweep her pain under the rug. She

didn't need another adult in her life to let her down, or aban-

don her. She needed someone to come through for her. She

needed someone to pick her up in their arms and love her back

to life. She needed a mommy to hold her and to get her

through this darkness that had dominated both of our lives.

Her life had had this tremendous domino effect on mine, and it

was time to set my anger about it aside. It wasn't her fault.

The blame didn't belong to her, no more than it was mine. I

needed to heal her and save her life. It was the only way to save my own.

I had an idea; a way to comfort her. It felt like a crazy idea to me when I first came up with it. But the more I thought about it, the more it made sense. When I was a little girl, I loved stuffed animals. They were soft, and cuddly. They made me feel safe. I decided that I was going to go out and buy a stuffed animal for her; for my inner child. I bought her a bunny. I named her Twinkles. Whenever my inner child was having a bad day, I would snuggle with Twinkles. I would take her with me in the car to run my errands on those tougher days. She brought that little girl peace and comfort. I told a few of my friends that I had purchased a stuffed animal for my inner child; absolutely certain that they would think I was crazy, but a few of these friends disclosed to me, that they too, had a stuffed animal of their own. So I guess it wasn't such a crazy idea after all! They had their reasons for having a stuffed animal and I had mine. Little Sarah, as I came to affectionately call her; loved Twinkles. I did my best to mother that broken little girl who lived inside my heart. But the more I allowed her to express her pain, the more she was taking over my adult universe. I realized that I had been relating to people in my life, more from Little Sarah's perspective and perception, than from that of my adult self. And it was becoming a destructive pattern. These conversations with a seven year old began to shift and change shape. I had spent many nights comforting her in the darkness; assuring her that I was doing everything I could to mend her world and her broken spirit. I was finally beginning to feel a difference inside of me. I felt a little less weighed down. I felt a little less lonely and a little less sad. I knew that I still had a long way to go on this journey of heal-ing, but I felt encouraged by my own bravery. I had already found the strength to share my story, to find a framework for healing and to open up the door to my past, and allow that broken child to come out and express her pain. Those precious

and heartbreaking conversations with that little girl; with sev-

en year old me, will never be forgotten. They will always hold

a special place in my heart. For they were among the first

steps I took on my path toward freedom. They were the first

awkward and beautiful steps of my awakening.

"You told me not to bite the hand that feeds me. But I didn't.

I bit the one that brought me so much pain.

I bit it over and over again,

until it didn't hurt to speak your name."

-Little girl speak

Chapter 8

A child in denial

Children are notorious for loving to hear stories. I wish that I could dedicate an entire chapter of my book to fairytales. When I was a little girl I loved fairytales, mainly because they were so different from the life that I knew. They were so far removed from the world that I lived in. It's strange how stories of non-existent whimsical creatures have the ability to make a child feel safe and grounded. Stories about things that could never take place in real life, have a way of making a child feel at peace in the real world, when their own reality becomes too difficult or overwhelming to think about. But children don't just love to hear stories; they love to tell stories too. This is an important part of childhood growth; discovering the power of creativity and imagination. When you are writing the story, you can create whatever kind of world you want. Oh how I wish I could dedicate this chapter, to all of the silly stories I made up when I was a little girl. That would feel much less uncomfortable to write about. But I think we all know that

Little girl speak

I'm not talking about fairytales here, am I? The stories I want to talk about in this chapter, have nothing to do with princesses, or super heroes with capes. I am talking about a more dangerous kind of story. The kind that starts out by saving a child's psyche, then later on destroys her adult self. I am talking about the stories that a traumatized child tells herself, in order to survive. The reality that I lived in, as a little girl who was being raped and brutalized, was too much for my mind to handle. As I've said before, children's brains are not equipped to handle trauma. So the child will tell herself stories about what's happening to her, in order to survive it. I told myself that what was happening to me, was probably happening to lots of other little girls too; that it was probably more normal than I realized. Quite simply put, I was a child in denial. I was in complete denial that I was being brutalized. I was in complete denial that what was happening to me, was affecting my development and my emotional health, far beneath the surface of my skin. I told myself anything I could to stay alive; to survive the hellish torture he bestowed upon me on a regular basis. And I'm torn here. I am so incredibly torn between two sides. There is this part of me that wants to stand up and praise that little girl. I know that the most important thing she could have done, was survive. So who in the hell cares what she told herself? She survived it, didn't she? But then there's this other part of me that recognizes how dangerous those lies and minimizations she told herself became, as she got older. The adult me has spent the better part of my life trying to change the past; trying to rewrite a history; a story that cannot be rewritten. Her childlike heart still dwells inside of me; that same heart that didn't want to believe the brutality of what she was experiencing. I spent decades of my life believing that I could somehow change the past, because she spent the better part of her life, lying to herself about the reality in which she lived in. The lies she told herself in order to survive had a ripple effect on my life. One that would not easily be disman-

tled, dismembered, or disassembled. These lies that she con-

structed in order to cope with her horrific reality, became so

entrenched and enmeshed in her brain, that I didn't know how

to unearth them. It was ingrained in her so deeply, to reject

reality; to remain in blissful denial of just how bad it all was.

And it left her with gaping wounds that began to bleed into

mine.

Looking back I see the truth now, in all of its glorious

frailty; that the only way for her to survive, was to live in a

perpetual state of denial. I don't judge her for it; I applaud her

efforts. She was pretty damn resilient and resourceful. But

what was I supposed to do, live in denial for the rest of my

life? If I had any hope of healing at all, I was going to have to

dismantle the lies she told herself and face the reality of what

she had experienced; of what I had experienced, in its fullness.

This was not a task for the faint of heart. I remember sitting in a therapy session, scared to death of this little girl inside of me. I was afraid of her. I was afraid of her feelings. I was afraid of her anger. I was afraid of her sadness. I was terrified, of her pain. I was so afraid, that if I pulled back the curtain, and showed her the reality of what she had endured, that she may never come back from it; that she may go into a place of sadness so deep, that I may never see her again. I was petrified that telling her the truth, might destroy what was left of her. And I didn't want to lose her for good; I didn't want her to go away, or to hate me. This is where survival story telling as I refer to it now, becomes dangerous. While it serves its purpose well for the child, it destroys the mind of the adult who is trying so desperately to heal. I realized that until I could help her face the reality of what she had endured, that there was no hope of me being able to move forward. She was a child who was in fierce denial of the truth. And I had to handle her with kid gloves, or I was going to lose the both of us.

144

Little girl speak

This stage of my healing process was confusing at best. I had already come to terms with the fact that I was raped. I had written my story down and I read it out loud. I had been trying to care for and nurture that little girl inside of me. I had answered so many of her questions and I had helped her to own her story; or so I thought. But what she had really come to terms with at this point, was only that first experience of abuse. She had accepted that it happened, but she minimized the ongoing rape and torture. She told herself that the fact that it had happened probably hundreds of times, was the same thing as if it had only happened once. It's not the same; not by a long shot. Now I am NOT minimizing the experience of a child who is only raped once, or the experience of a child who is molested, without being raped. Any type of sexual assault is horrific for a child to endure. It is severely damaging to their emotional and physical well-being. What I am talking about here, is not about any type of comparison; but rather

145

about acceptance of the truth; her truth. Whatever your truth

is; whatever reality you lived through, it is so important for

you to understand that a vital part of your healing, is going to

be dismantling the lies you told yourself as a child, to mini-

mize what you experienced. Just as I did, it is important for

you to honor that lie, because it is the very thing that sustained

that broken little girl inside of you. It was the core belief that

she clung to, that led to her survival; and so you must honor it,

and her. But continuing to believe her lie; continuing to mini-

mize what you experienced, will not serve either one of you

now. This stage of the healing process was so incredibly diffi-

cult for me, because it wasn't just about telling her the truth,

and slowly forcing her to accept it. This stage of healing, in-

volved a lot of grieving and loss. You see, when you begin to

dismantle the lies of minimization and denial, you not only

have to accept the horrific reality that you lived through per-

vasive torture and abuse, but you also have to grieve the loss of a childhood that you never had; and one that you can never get back, or do over again. I remember being blindsided, by the grief that accompanied this stage of my healing. I wanted a do over so badly. I wanted to go back in time and rewrite her history. After I yelled about the injustice of it all; after I raged about how unfair it was that she never got to really be a kid; after the anger subsided, the grief set in. I remember laying on my bathroom floor, just thrashing around and screaming in emotional pain. I was crawling out of my skin with grief. If you had asked me in that very moment, if this healing process was worth it, I would have probably told you that it wasn't. I would have probably told you, that I wished I had never opened pandora's box, and that I had left the damn thing up on a high shelf, far out of my reach. Looking back on that time now, while I wouldn't want to relive it, seeing how it connected with the next steps of my healing, and knowing where those steps brought me to; I can tell you now, that it was definitely worth every moment of agony I endured, to get

here. Grieving the loss of a stolen childhood that was domi-

nated by torture and abuse, was one of the hardest things that I

have ever done. It was so incredibly painful. But you know

what? It wasn't as painful as surviving it in the first place. And

it wasn't as painful as my life would be right now, had I de-

cided not to heal; had I decided to allow my fear of accepting

the truth, to keep me trapped as a helpless child, in denial. She

had no power over her world; not a shred of control. But her

reality isn't mine. And continuing to live like it was, would

have ultimately destroyed the both of us.

Little girl speak

"She's a hurricane child, who was buried alive.

Covered in all of the mud, from the grave that she clawed her

way up and out of; from the horror she left behind.

You say you don't know how to deal with a soul like that;

one that's been to hell and back. Well honey, neither do I.

And you're not the one, who has to live within its bones.

This heart ain't yours. It's mine."

-Little girl speak

"I've been chasing after freedom, for what feels like eternity.

All I know, is I've got this war deep inside,

and it won't let go of me."

-Little girl speak

Chapter 9

The messy middle

Little girl speak

This next phase of the healing process, will probably

feel like the scariest. Why? Because it's the longest and most

unpredictable phase. You feel like you're living in limbo, most

days. You aren't healed up, but you're also no longer numb

and shut down. You are highly in tune with what you're feel-

ing, and why. And that can be a difficult thing to manage, as

you try to maintain your daily living; the normalcy of life. My

definition of normal has drastically changed over the years.

And that god awful messy middle is where I found myself. I

discovered who I was, and what I was made of, during this

phase of my healing. Being someone who is somewhat of a

control freak, this phase of my healing really freaked me out at

first. I found myself often torn between moving forward, and

wanting to quit and run back. The thing is, that running back

to the things that broke you, won't heal you. The things that

put you in the cage in the first place, could never be the things

that will set you free. And so, I began to navigate

what I refer to, as the "messy middle."

The darkness and numbness that had engulfed my life for as far back as I remember, were beginning to dissipate more and more, the further along I got in my healing process, and in my self-awareness. One would think that I would take comfort, in the fact that I was growing and healing. I was seeing signs of life in that little girl again, for the first time since before the trauma. I had spent so much time in therapy, slowly processing her pain. Dissecting it; studying it. Separating the truth from the lies that she told herself, in order to survive; those creeds that she lived by. This process would come to change the negative tapes, that had been playing over and over again inside my head, for decades of my life. But getting through this phase of my healing, was going to take every ounce of grit and determination I had left, inside of me. I felt like I was sitting in a boat all by myself, in the middle of the ocean. The storms weren't raging, but the seas weren't calm.

And if I looked behind me, I couldn't see the shore anymore. And if I looked in front of me, I couldn't see any land; there was nothing in sight. I had no way of knowing where I was going, or how long it was going to take me to get there. And I was terrified. The pain and numbness that I had felt all of those years was awful, but it was predictable. Though I was emotionally unhealthy and shut down during those years, I knew who I was. I knew I was stuck, but at least I didn't feel lost, and unable to see where I was going. This phase of my healing left me feeling utterly lost and confused about what would come next. The unknown of it all, felt so scary to me. This is the stage of the healing process, when you will most want to give up; when you will most want to throw in the towel, jump out of that boat and swim for your life back to the abandoned shores from which you came. But don't. Refuse to listen to that voice that's screaming in your head, telling you that you're not gonna make it. You will make it. I can promise you that. And this is how you know, that you're getting it right; that you're healing. When you want to run backwards, but long to move forward, you are in the right place. You are in the exact space where you are meant to be. That's how you know you're doing it right; when you've gotten yourself out in the middle of nowhere, with no end in sight.

This is the phase of the healing process, that everyone tries to skip over; but it is imperative to your healing, that you don't. So many survivors; myself included, started out this process with the core belief, that if we owned our stories; if we shared them out loud, that we would be catapulted into this amazing place, where we felt almost instantly patched up, and healed. Realizing that this was not going to be my reality, was devastating. I mean, it's difficult enough to speak about this pain out loud. It's difficult enough to disclose our stories of abuse, to another human being. You would think that some-how something magic would happen, in response to our sheer bravery, in opening up and sharing our stories out loud. I kept waiting for this magical portal to open up, and transport me to the finish line. "I'm done." I thought. "I made the decision to heal. I shared my story out loud. I spent so much time in therapy by now, processing so much trauma and pain. I've had flashbacks and nightmares of the abuse. I've spent nights laying alone on my bathroom floor, because the cold temperature of the tile somehow felt comforting against the side of my face." I truly believed that I should be "healed up" by now. But I wasn't; I wasn't even close. And I felt like I was doing something wrong. At this time, I was attending a church that I am now no longer a part of. Churches tend to be places where these issues are not discussed very often, and when they are, they are usually met with phrases such as: "Well if you pray about it more, God will just heal you." This was the mentality of my church community. As I began to move further along in my healing process, I began to feel safe enough to let a circle of people in; to let them know and see the real me; the me who

was fighting so hard, for my freedom from the past. There are

memories that I will never forget; memories of friends circling

around me, and holding me as I sobbed. I carry those moments

with me wherever I go. As painful as those moments were for

me, there was a beauty in them. It was a stunningly beautiful

image, of what humanity can look like when we choose to

deeply care for another; when we make the decision to join

someone else in their agony, or allow them to join us in ours.

Those moments, were humanity at its best. But there was a

darker side of that church community; one that was filled with

judgement, and ignorance. There were individuals in that

church who truly believed, that I should be able to pray one

prayer and be healed of all the trauma in my past. And when

that didn't work, because it isn't possible for it to work; they

shamed me and made me feel as if I was doing something

wrong, because I wasn't healed yet. Most of the time that I

spent within that church community, I lived in constant fear

that I was a failure; that there was something inherently wrong

with me, because I wasn't healed yet. And so, I made a very

difficult decision. I began to distance myself from that com-

munity and eventually I left. During this messy middle of my

healing process, I had come to realize a few things. The first,

is that I had allowed the opinions of others to rule my life and

my mind, since the trauma had entered into my world. He had

penetrated my body and my mind. He controlled what I did,

the way I thought, and the way that I viewed myself. And that

set up a pattern in my life, of allowing others to control my

thoughts and my opinions of myself, along the way. I didn't

want to do that anymore; I didn't want to allow the opinions of

others, to steer my own. It felt so strange to me, that I was be-

coming stronger and stronger, in the middle of the ocean on

that boat; still unable to see either shoreline. But I was. For the

first time in my life, I was beginning to develop thoughts and opinions of my own. For the first time in my life, I was beginning to see my worth, and it felt amazing. For the first time in my life, I began to discover what I believed in, the things that I stood for, and I began to stand firm in those things. I realized that somehow, I was digging roots for myself right there, in the middle of the ocean; in the middle of nowhere. I was becoming this tall tree, sprouting up, right out of the water; land out of sight. In the messy middle, is where I found my footing for the very first time. In the glorious messy middle, is where I began to feel alive.

"Remember that story about the really brave warrior woman who decided to heal, and then gave up and closed the door? Neither do I. Keep going. You will move beyond this tough space that you're in. I know, because you've already done it, Little One. You've done it, more than once before. It is the fierceness in your years, not the absence of your tears, that is going to win you this war."

-Little girl speak

Chapter 10

Setbacks and pitfalls

Ok. Are you listening? Are you sitting still, and paying attention? Because this part is really important. I went through this process pretty blindly, and I fell into some setbacks and pitfalls. Some of them proved to be necessary for my continued growth and healing, but some of them were not. I am going to do my best in this chapter, to offer you nuggets of wisdom from my own experience. It is my hope that in me sharing about the many, many times I've stumbled through the darkness and crawled back out into the light on my hands and knees, that you will be able to reflect back on this chapter; that you will remember it, as you get to this phase in your own healing journey. It is my hope, that by me sharing my stories of falling, that it will empower you to rise.

Setbacks, setbacks, and more setbacks. These are to be expected, during this process of remaking and reshaping yourself, from the inside out. I want you to have a set of realistic expectations here, for yourself. I want you to avoid some of the pitfalls that I fell into, that led to some really difficult

spaces that I found myself trapped in. It can be hard to unfold

yourself again, when you've gotten yourself into a tight space.

I became the master, of corning my own heart; of setting my-

self up for failure, by expecting too much from myself too

quickly. I had a set of rules and expectations that I had laid out

for myself, and I was determined to live by them. And when

they proved to not pan out, I felt devastated. One of the big-

gest nuggets of wisdom that I an offer you from my own expe-

rience, is this: BE GENTLE WITH YOURSELF. Let me say

that again, because I really need to know that you know how

important this is. Please, I am begging you, BE GENTLE

WITH YOURSELF. It took you years to survive what hap-

pened to you, and you aren't going to be able to heal over-

night. You spent years building walls around your heart, and

cultivating coping skills that got you through. And no matter

how hard you fight, this process takes time. You won't be able to dismantle the negative tapes inside your head in a week, or a month, or even in a year. You won't be able to pick up new coping skills, like French fries at a drive thru McDonalds. These tools aren't "made to order." This process doesn't happen quickly, and it isn't supposed to. Accepting this, was really difficult for me. I wish that I could tell you that these setbacks and pitfalls only happened during the lengthy messy middle of my healing journey, but that simply isn't the case. I would come out into the light for a while, and then fall backwards into the darkness again. Part of that back and forth is going to happen no matter what; it's just a part of normal living, and we will talk about that more in depth in a few minutes. But what I'm talking about right now, is not the normal ups and downs of life. What I'm referring to, is the rollercoaster that I strapped myself onto unknowingly, by not having realistic goals, or realistic expectations for myself. Before you can run, you have to walk. And before you can walk, you have to crawl. I wanted to run. I wanted to take off running.

Once I saw the light for the first time, I thought I would never

look back. Once I felt the warmth of the sun shining down on

my face, I couldn't bear the thought that it would ever rain

again. Once I had finally found a way to become present in my

body, and present in my surroundings, I was sure that I was

well on my way to being whole. I had no idea, that a back and

forth tug of war between light and darkness, was about to

completely dominate my universe.

My therapist tried to tell me in a nice way, that my

quest for freedom wasn't over. "You're gonna struggle again,"

She would tell me. I sat there glaring at her, with a look of

frustration and pensiveness. I rolled my eyes and flung my

arms across my chest in a heaving motion. "So I guess we

must be in the sullen teenager phase of our inner child healing

now huh?" She said, half-jokingly. "Ha Ha." I said. By this

time I had been going to therapy for a long while, and I knew that Ali was not in any way, trying to make light of my trauma. She was simply stating a fact, and she was right! When I had first come to her for therapy, I was a wife and a mother of two children, but I myself on the inside in many ways, was still a child. There was a part of me that was frozen and suspended in time, as a seven year old little girl. The whole framework of my healing process was this idea of growing up that child inside of me, step by step. I guess this was the next phase in my healing process; the sullen teenager phase. I don't think this was Ali's particularly favorite phase. Teenagers are difficult creatures sometimes. It's funny to me now, as I look back on it, because I felt like I was leading a double life. At home, I was a wife and a mother. I kept my home immaculately clean; I still do, because I'm somewhat of a neat freak. Ok, I'm probably a little bit OCD, but I've made my peace with it. When I was home, I was taking care of my children and my husband, and my house. I was cleaning, doing laundry,

running errands, and driving the kids to various playdates and
doctor's appointments. I won't say that I spent much time
cooking, because I'm not very good at it. My husband is the
cook in our household. But you get what I'm trying to say here
right? When I was at home, I was a wife and a mother. I did
wifey things. I did mother things. But when I stepped into
Ali's office, it's like I stepped through a portal, back in time. I
would immediately take off my wife and mother hat at the
door, flop on her couch, let out a sigh or a grunt of frustration,
perhaps cry a little, or throw pillows at her if I didn't like what
she had to say. (Yes I did actually did throw pillows at her
sometimes, but in a silly way.) I would often take off my
shoes, and sometimes I would even bring a cozy blanket with
me. And there I sat; body strewn across her couch, draping
over the edges of her dark gray sofa. I was dripping with teenage attitude and angst. I was a ball of anxiety and frustration,
and I did absolutely nothing, to hide it. Ali's office became

167

the one place in the world, where I could be imperfect; where I could be me. And at that time, ME, was a very fluid concept. For decades, I had almost no control over anything, and my feelings and opinions didn't seem to matter, so I stopped sharing them; even with myself. I had spent the better part of my life, enslaved to this belief that there was nothing particularly special or unique about me. And it had been ingrained in my brain from a very young age, that I was unworthy of love. Not only was I in the sullen teenager phase of my healing journey, but I had no idea who in the hell I was. I didn't really know what my opinions were about different things, because I had never really been allowed to have opinions. I didn't know how I felt about most things, because my feelings were stifled for years. I had spent the better part of my life, choking back any shred of emotion that I felt. Part of this process of healing my inner child; of growing her up inside of me, was having to re-learn how to feel again. I had been numbed out and shut down

168

emotionally for so long, that I didn't know how to think for

myself, or how to stand my ground when I did finally form

opinions about something. Teenagers are fickle creatures, and

in that moment I was the epitome of fickle. I had to learn how

to regulate my emotions. We will talk more about that, toward

the end of the book. For right now, I want to focus our atten-

tion to my mishaps; to the setbacks and pitfalls that I fell into;

both the necessary ones, and the not so necessary ones.

So here I was, torn between two worlds; one that was

my daily reality, and the portal that I stepped into once or

twice a week for an hour, when I entered Ali's office. Merging

these two worlds together, felt like an impossible task. I'm

sure that you've felt like this before. Maybe you feel like this

now; like you're torn between two worlds. The world in which

you are forced to live in every day on the outside, and the

world in which you are forced to live in every day, on the in-

side. My outside and inside world, were WORLDS APART,

and I had no idea what to do, to merge them together. But I knew that I needed to join them together; somehow, I needed to unite them, into one world; into one WHOLE person, instead of two HALVES. If I was going to heal, it was going to take ALL of me; all of who I was, to make it happen. I got stuck for a while, in the sullen teenager phase. Getting stuck was definitely a pitfall that I continuously fell into, over and over again. You're gonna get stuck; that is to be expected. But STAYING STUCK, is something entirely different. And I was STAYING STUCK, a LOT. Here is what getting stuck looked like for me. I'm not sure what it looks like for you, but I'm almost certain that we will have some common ground here. Getting stuck for me, looked like obsession. If I couldn't stop obsessing about a certain aspect of my personality. I remember thinking at one point that I talk too much. I would focus on it, and I would make an effort not to speak as often. It caused me to be very self-conscious in social situations, and even at home in my own house, with my own family. Obsessing over personality traits, often left me feeling stuck. Triggers, also left me feeling stuck. If I heard a story that sounded similar to my own trauma, I would begin to get flashbacks again, and I would feel stuck. Getting stuck can look different and feel different, for each of us. But the common threads of being stuck, are feelings of hopelessness; a feeling that things will never get better again. Feelings of overwhelming shame; that somehow this must be your fault, since you aren't healed yet and everyone else around you, appears to be so "happy" and so "well put together." Comparison is another HUGE thing that left me stuck quite often. Comparing your life and your experiences, to that of someone who has not experienced this trauma, will leave you feeling utterly exhausted and mentally drained. In fact, comparing yourself to basically anyone else, will leave you feeling sad and discontented with yourself and with your life path. I got stuck a LOT, when I compared my

171

life to someone else's whom I perceived to have a "great life" or an "ideal situation." Getting stuck is unavoidable. It's going to happen. But staying stuck, is a choice. And believe me when I tell you, that it's not a choice you want to make, no matter how good you think it feels in the moment. When you're stuck, it's important to acknowledge it. Knowledge is power. You cannot heal, what you aren't willing to feel. Allow yourself to feel the pain. Allow yourself to acknowledge that you're stuck, and sit with that feeling for a moment or two, or twenty. The whole point of this healing process, is learning how to feel our emotions again; so avoiding the difficult emotions that come up during this process, is about as pointless as swinging a baseball bat, when no one is pitching you a ball. I know it sucks. Sadness SUCKS. Anger SUCKS. Being stuck, SUCKS. But until and unless you are willing to acknowledge these difficult feelings, you will remain stuck. And that sucks worst of all; believe me. Staying stuck, SUCKS.

Little girl speak

I guess I should talk about how to not stay stuck, in order to explain what staying stuck looks like, and why for a
while, it was actually my preferable choice. Choosing to come
out of being stuck is sometimes not that difficult. It can be as
simple as taking a hot bath, or going for a jog, or calling a
friend on the phone for some support and or laughter. Sometimes those little things that make us feel safe, can jolt us right
out of being stuck. But other times, it's more difficult. There is
a fine line between allowing yourself to feel your emotions,
and getting stuck in them. There is a delicate dance to it. It's
like an art; one that you will get better at, with time. Practice
makes perfect. This isn't the part of the healing process where
I "mastered" the art of regulating my emotions. That came later on, and I promise we will talk about that before the pages of
this book run out. But in this moment, I want to zero in on
some things you can do to help yourself, when you are feeling
stuck. I asked some friends to give me lists of things that they

do when they are feeling stuck in sadness, stuck in depression, or stuck in anxiety. Some of their answers were the same, but many of their answers were different, and it reminded me of how each of us, are so intricately unique. Something that might be so soothing to one person, can be completely anxiety provoking to another. But our similarities far outweigh our differences, when it comes to the NEED to feel safe. All of us as human beings, want to feel safe. We all have things that we do, that ground us and center us. Here are some of the things that my friends do, that help them get unstuck:

Going for a walk

Taking a long shower

Folding the laundry (yes, I was shocked by this one too)

Crying with a friend

Watching a sad movie

Laughing with a friend

Watching a funny TV show

Little girl speak

Playing with their pet

Going for a jog

Running on the treadmill

Curling up on the couch with a blanket and a good book

Going for a long drive

Listening to music

Meditating

Writing

Singing

Sleeping (never underestimate the power, of a nap)

Taking photos of nature

Taking a bubble bath

Playing with their children

Seeing their therapist

Knitting

Word search puzzles

Playing the lottery

Yoga

Shopping

Getting a manicure

Going to the gym

Getting a massage

Playing basketball

Video games

Gardening

I could go on and on, but I will stop there. Those are just some of the things that my friends do, when they are stressed out, and STUCK. Does anything on this list resonate with you? If so, maybe it would be a good idea to write them down, so that the next time you're feeling stuck, you can pull out your list, and try to do some of the things on it! Maybe you can even add some additional things to the list, that are unique stress relievers for you! Maybe some of the things on this list don't seem very soothing to you. That's the beauty of humanity. We all have things that make us feel grounded and safe, when we're not feeling so well. It's so important to know what things will help jolt us out of being stuck, before we actually get stuck. I didn't know what would help me, until it was too late; until I was already stuck. And once you get yourself into that tiny small corner, and you're feeling weighed down by the world and insignificant, not having a plan is not a good idea. I was reading some interesting things about old mines. One of the first things they did when constructing them, was build an exit. They made sure, before they went deep underground, that there was a way out. Before you enter, make sure that you have built your exit. Let me rephrase this in a way that will stick out in your mind, because this is so crucially important, to not staying stuck. Build your EXIT, before your ENTRANCE. Know what your triggers are; the things that are going to make you feel stuck, and have a plan in place; things you can do that will help you to become unstuck again. Don't do what I did; don't wait until you're stuck, to try and figure out what makes you feel safe and grounded. Be proactive in your healing. Sit down and write out your list, or make a mental list and embed it into your brain. I don't care what form your list is in, just as long as you have one; just as long as you know where it is. Because I can promise you, that you are going to need it.

So there I was, STUCK. Undeniably and utterly STUCK. I had no idea how to become unstuck, and even worse; I wasn't entirely sure that I wanted to know. I was getting stuck so often, that it was becoming my preferable choice, to remain stuck. It took so much effort and work to get myself unstuck; only to circle around and end up back in the same damn place over and over again. "What was the point?" I thought. What was the point of getting myself unstuck, if I was just going to end up getting stuck again? I'm sure you've heard the saying before, that "the definition of insanity is repeating the same behavior, expecting to get different results." I felt like I was on a gerbil wheel, just spinning and spinning and I couldn't get off. But the problem wasn't my healing. I wasn't getting stuck, because I was feeling. I wasn't setting myself up for pitfalls by continuing to do this healing work. I blamed being stuck, on my bright idea to heal. I blamed being stuck, on my inability to achieve perfection. But the issue wasn't my healing; it was the tools I was choosing to utilize, in order to make myself feel better. It was clear, that they weren't working. I was falling down over and over again, and getting stuck over and over again. Something had to change, or I wouldn't be able to move onto the next phase of my healing journey. And so I made the decision to examine the tools in my toolbox. And guess what I figured out? I needed to make a list; MY list of the things that make ME feel grounded and safe, no matter what's going on around me. The tools I had been using were other people's, not my own.

And like everything else in this process, figuring out what my tools were, would be both unique and complicated.

I want to close out this chapter, by talking about setbacks for a moment. For me, pitfalls and setbacks have always been kind of intertwined. I fall into an emotional pit of dirt, I get stuck, and then I feel like I took two steps backwards in my healing process; hence the SETBACK. Feeling like you've had a setback and feeling stuck, can often feel the same, and even BE the same. There is no way to avoid setbacks in this process. They will happen; of that much, I am certain. But we do have an element of choice, within its constraints. We cannot choose whether or not we have these setbacks and pitfalls; they are like I said; inevitable. But what we can choose, is the degree to which we allow them to manipulate us, and wreak havoc on our bodies, and our minds. Another nugget of wisdom that I want to offer you, for this phase of your healing process is this: IT ALL MATTERS. Every piece of your pain, matters. Every piece of your joy, matters. Every shred of hope

that you manage to feel and grab onto for dear life, it matters.

The further along you get in your healing process, the more

hope and the more joy you will begin to experience again. It

will make you feel alive, in ways that you never thought pos-

sible. Hold onto those moments, when you feel enveloped by

that hope. Soak in them. Take them in. Remember what they

feel like, so that when the setbacks and pitfalls inevitably

come, you will remain strong enough to keep going; to keep

putting one foot in front of the other; to keep fighting, for your

freedom.

"Who are you really? And who in the hell am I?
And what can be left of this pain I've been holding?
I tucked it away, in a place deep inside. I plastered on a fake
smile for as long as I can remember; for decades of my life.
But today I woke up so exhausted and deflated. I'm so damn
tired of running, and there's no place left to hide. My bones
have grown so tired here, and I'm running out of time. Breathe
into me. Save me. He sucked all the air from within my lungs.
I have so many words still left to say; so much damn unwritten
pain. And there are so many songs still left to be sung. And all
of my questions still hang here in the balance. They've all
gone unanswered as I stand here in silence; as I lay here in
chains, and forcibly hold my tongue. And I'm not gonna stop
fighting, until I find what I'm looking for; until I've exhausted
every option; until I've pried open every door. I am deserving
of these answers, and I am fiercely hell bent on getting them.
It's a pity really; the way you used to own me. The way you
used to hold my silence. The way you used to cradle my fear. I
lost count, of how many times you abused me. You just left
me there for dead; day after day; year after year. I used to
cower in the corner and beg you to stop, as you raped me and
dragged me across the bedroom floor. But I took my life back!
I found my strength and my voice. They were buried deep
inside me. And I can promise you this: in spite of the pain that
engulfs my soul daily, I will never stop opening this door.
I will never stop fighting for my healing and my freedom.
I will not be silent anymore."

-Little girl speak

Chapter 11

The empowered and angry adult

Little girl speak

This next phase of my healing journey was probably one of my favorites, because it was the first time in my life, that I had strong opinions about anything. It was the first time in my life, that I felt like I was actually beginning to LIVE. I felt WOKE. My eyes were opened, not only to my own suffering, but I was keenly aware of those who were suffering all around me, and I knew that I needed to do something about it. Plainly and simply, I was angry. I was extremely angry, about a lot of things. This was the first time in my life, that I felt safe enough and free enough in my own skin, to express my anger. I had so much anger, just teeming beneath the surface ALL THE TIME, for a good long while. And finding healthy ways to manage that anger and to express it, would prove to be yet another hurdle; another wall, for me to have to climb; or in my case, claw my way up and over. By this time, I was good and ready to conquer the world. I felt empowered, by my own de-termination to heal. Resilience seeped through my pores, like water. But I knew that if I didn't find a way to channel my anger, that I was going to drown in it. I decided to write yet another list. If you haven't figured it out by now, lists are something that make me feel very safe, and grounded. So here was my list of grievances if you will; the list of all the things that were making me so angry at the world: The loss of the childhood that had been stolen from me. The fact that this horror happened to SO MANY GIRLS. The fact that law enforcement treated rape victims like criminals. The fact that the church community somehow believed that prayer alone, could heal a rape victim completely. The fact that the church community actually judged rape victims and told them that it was their fault, that they weren't healed yet, because they weren't praying hard enough. The fact that ignorant people who did not understand anything about trauma, would tell me and other survivors as well, that these experiences were all in the past, and that all we needed to do was leave them in the past, and

185

move on with our lives. I was angry and enraged at the injustice of it all. But more than that, I was angry because I knew what it took, for me to begin to heal. I knew how incredibly painful this healing process was, and how much courage and bravery it took for me to be willing to even try to heal. What would happen to other survivors; if just like me, were met with such judgement and callousness? Would they know to keep going? Would they inherently know deep inside, that there are good people in this world, who will come alongside them and love them through this process? Would they have the willingness inside, to hold onto hope and keep speaking their truth; or would they reclaim their silence and shut down forever? It dawned on me, that this process I was going through, was not just important for me; but it was also important to share it with other survivors. I wasn't quite healed up enough yet, to do so. But I knew at some point that I would need to, and that gave me a new sense of purpose. My healing

186

wasn't just about me anymore, it was about every survivor who would come across my path. It was about choosing to be fueled and empowered by my anger, instead of being controlled by it. This caused a huge cosmic shift inside of me. I began to see a bigger picture here, of what I needed to do. And even though I wasn't ready to do it yet, I knew that the time would come, when I would be. And that gave me hope. Coming to terms with, and connecting to your anger, is a HUGE step, and an AMAZING sign on your journey. It feels strange to say that you should feel happy and at peace, that you are enraged and angry, but in this case, it's true. It's a sign; a huge and glaring sign, that you are beginning to move forward; that you are beginning to really do this difficult healing work. I remember standing in my kitchen one morning; cup of coffee in hand, birds chirping outside my window, and I took in a long deep breath, and I let it out slowly, as I watched the birds hopping from branch to branch. I was aware that I was present in that moment. I was present in my body. I felt the heat from the coffee mug, sending warmth through my fingertips and my hands. I felt the taste of this glorious cup of coffee, as it trickled down my throat. The chirping of the birds was echoing in my head, like a heaven song. I felt the tile floor; cold and dense beneath my feet, as I wiggled my toes against their grainy surface. And for that brief moment, time stood still, as I was connecting with the world around me. For that brief moment my anger subsided, and I was completely at peace. A new knowledge and truth was born inside me, in that very moment. A knowledge and recognition, that no matter what was going on around me, or even inside me; that I could find these moments of peace within the storm; that I was fully capable of finding my calm, amidst the waves of emotion that I was grappling with on a daily basis. This truth was born that day, and it's something that I've held onto ever since. No matter what chaos ensues around us, or even inside us as a result of our trauma and our healing work, we can find and cultivate moments of peace, that will keep us going. We can search for nuggets of wisdom and hope and self-awareness to hold onto, as the dark clouds continue to form overhead; as the storm continues to rage.

Something else that started to happen for me in this phase of my healing journey, was that the blame and the shame, were beginning to take their proper places. I shook my head in awe, at how far I'd come. I had walked into Ali's office that first day, a completely broken, and terrified jumbled up mess. Now here I was over two years later, embarking on what I felt, was the last leg of my healing journey, and I was proud. I was so damn proud of myself, for the first time in my life. I was proud of all I had accomplished so far, in my quest to find healing and freedom. I was encouraged by this deep desire that was growing stronger and stronger every day, to build an empire of empowerment; to find a place in the world,

189

where I could nestle in, and get to work empowering and in-spiring other survivors, to begin to heal and find their voice again, like I was. I knew that I was on the cusp of doing such work, but that I wasn't quite ready yet. But I saw all these signs of life; all these signs of progress and healing within my-self. And like a proud little peacock, I strutted my feathers. I stepped out into my world every day, armed with determina-tion, strength, power, and hope. Now all of these things had been there the whole time, from the very beginning; I just didn't see them for what they were. They had felt more like weakness and frailty. They had felt more like hopelessness and fear. I realized now looking back, that I was brave; that I was resilient, and that I had the strength and grit inside of me, to face whatever was coming next. When you get to this phase of your healing process, allow your anger and your empower-ment to channel itself into the MAYBES and the WHAT IFS. Speak truth to yourself, as you move into this place in your healing journey. MAYBE you WILL heal. MAYBE you can

make a DIFFERENCE in the lives of other SURVIVORS by

sharing YOUR story when you're ready to. WHAT IF you

find your joy and your peace again? WHAT IF it's entirely

possible? WHAT IF your journey can make a difference in the

lives of so many others? When children are little, they dream

about being different things when they grow up. They are no-

where near ready to leave their parent's nest, and become who

they were meant to be; but that doesn't stop them from dream-

ing, nor should it. Just because you're not ready to figure out

what your journey could do; not only you but for others, that

shouldn't stop you from dreaming about it; from thinking

about it. Dreaming about what being further healed will feel

like for you, is such an important thing to do. It is such an im-

portant step. It is a mile marker in this process. It is a huge

sign, that you are continuing to heal; that you are continuing to

work through the most difficult moments of your life, in order to prepare yourself for the possibility and belief, that healing is possible. It is a sign that you are preparing your heart, to step into the joy and the peace, and the fullness of life, that awaits you at the end of this long, dark tunnel of healing. Believe me warrior, your pain is worth feeling. Your heart is worth healing. You have no idea of the magic, that is about to swiftly awaken inside of you. Hold onto hope, and keep going brave soul. For your spring, is about to come.

Little girl speak

"Twisted up inside this storm, I've no place left to go. My blood stained hands are tired and worn, with nothing left to show. These aching bones protrude from skin, that faded long ago. It's hard, when you got nothing to live for; when no place, feels like home. All alone, on the darkest path I wandered; incomplete, and by myself. Bumping into sticks and stones, as I morphed into someone else. Creatures all around me suck the air, from within my lungs. I'm racing, to hold onto all the oxygen I have left, as my heart gives out, and I slowly, come undone. Laying on the cold hard ground, just a shadow of who I used to be. Mask torn off, without a sound; to reveal all that's left of me. I spent my childhood running from monsters, that were lurking in my bed. While visions of what real love should look like, were daydreams, inside my head. I starved my body, until it disappeared; until it showed the scars, from within. I took that razor, intending to feel; as I cut away, all my skin. With demons clawing at my walls, I couldn't stand the sound, of their shouts; so desperately trying, to rid myself of them; trying so hard, to let them out. I fought so hard, to be her again; that little girl, who was innocent and free. But all these chains that weigh me down, are drowning the life out of me. She sung her songs, by the hour glass; the same one, that brings her no comfort now. For he would always come and find her there, by the time, the sand ran out. As songs of chaos, now defined her existence; no more happy little girl, with a smile on her face. Her heart, now shattered; her soul, now broken. Her innocence destroyed; forever gone, without a trace. She fought so hard, in the reckoning; in facing these demons, that wounded her soul. But no matter how many times she's defeated them; she knows, they still have control. She is doomed to a life, of history repeated. She knows now, there's no such thing, as moving forward; that there's no room left in her heart, to believe it. No matter how fiercely, she fights this war, within herself; she will always be

Little girl speak

trapped, inside this nightmare; inside this space; inside this room, that holds everything, that she still lacks. From this symphony of black; you can't run, you can't hide, you can't shield yourself no longer. And no matter what they've told you; you're never going back."

-Little girl speak

Chapter 12

The darkest night

Little girl speak

This was the phase that I DIDN'T see coming. I NEVER saw it coming, and it knocked the wind and the life, right out of me. My hope is that if I can share this most difficult phase of my healing journey with you, that perhaps you will be a little more gentle with yourself than I was with myself, when it happened to me. I like things that fit together; things that make sense; things that can be completed. I love circles. I love how they don't have any sharp edges. I love how content and complete they look. I love how they seem to serve as a fortress; how they keep things out, and protect what's inside. The only fortress that I ever had around me, was the wall that I had built myself; that thirty foot high wall, that had separated me from the world. What I realized as my healing progressed, was that that wall had actually even separated me, from myself. It had served as a barrier between me, and my authenticity. And I know, I know. You're probably thinking to yourself: "Didn't she already knock that wall down? Shouldn't she have been able to step into her authenticity by NOW?" The answer

to the first question, is YES I had already knocked that god-

forsaken wall down. But the answer to the second question, is

far more complicated. I myself firmly believed at this point,

that I was healed. I adamantly believed that I was healed. I

believed that I had stepped into my authenticity and that life

was going to be just fine, from this point on. I never expected

to feel a darkness come over me again. And this wasn't just

any darkness. This was the DARKEST darkness that I had

EVER felt in my life. Now in reality, I'm sure that things ac-

tually felt darker to me when I was a little girl; when I was

surviving the abuse itself. But I guess what happened, is that

because I had experienced so much light, and so much joy by

now; since I had made the decision to go through this healing

process, that when this darkness came and hit me like an anvil

out of nowhere, it felt like the worst and scariest darkness in

the world. I was so completely blindsided by it, and I had no idea what to do. I was just moving along on my healing journey and BAM there it was; sheer and utter DARKNESS. A depression came over me that I couldn't explain. An anxiety took over my body that I could barely control. I stopped eating again. I stopped sleeping again. I found myself staring blankly out my window in the morning, as fatigue coursed through my veins, and caused my body to ache, from head to toe. Why was this happening to me? What caused this to happen, and how on earth could I fix it? Had all of this healing work that I had done, been for NOTHING? I sat in my bedroom, with a clean pile of laundry fresh from the dryer surrounding me, just waiting to be folded. I formed it into a circle, then I laid in the empty middle; knees tucked up tight under my chin; arms around my legs as tightly as I could squeeze them. Then I closed my eyes, and tried to just center myself, and to breathe; to just breathe. Somehow I knew in that moment, that everything would eventually be ok again; it had to be. I had worked too long and too hard, for it not to be. I didn't know why this was happening to me, or how to fix it; but I was fiercely determined, to figure it out.

As I began to think more deeply, about what had been happening in my therapy sessions lately, I started to slowly uncover why this dark night of the soul, had come to plague me. It was in fact, NOT out of nowhere at all. Our minds have a way of blocking out certain experiences or aspects of our trauma, until we are ready to deal with them; until we are ready to handle them, without losing our minds quite frankly. We know that these experiences are there, but we continue to push them down, and shove them out of the way. We try our hardest, not to think about them. We tell ourselves that we don't need to discuss every putrid horrific detail of our trauma, in order to heal. We try to navigate our way around a few of the "minor details," because we think that it won't make a dif-ference to discuss them; that it would only bring more harm to us than good, to let them out into the open; out into the harsh light of day. The pieces of your trauma that you would find most upsetting to talk about, are the most IMPORTANT pieces of all. Telling yourself that these things are just "minor details," is a continuation of the lies you told yourself as a child, in order to survive; and those lies won't serve you now. There were aspects of my trauma that I NEVER wanted to talk about; NOT EVER; NOT TO ANYONE. But somewhere along the way, I realized that EVERY MOMENT MATTERS; that EVERY DETAIL MATTERS. If you were putting a puzzle together, and you left five or six pieces out, the puzzle wouldn't look complete. It would look so strange, to have missing pieces. Healing from trauma is the same concept. You need EVERY piece of the puzzle, to heal. Even the pieces that you don't think are significant. Even the pieces that you don't want to talk about; ESPECIALLY those ones. When I sat down and thought about it, I knew exactly why this darkness had come over me. I was TRIGGERED. I was triggered in a way that I had never been before; on a deeper level than I had ever experienced. And to my surprise and dismay, even with all of the tools I had gained along the way in my emotional toolbox, it wasn't enough to stop this darkness from coming. It wasn't enough, to keep this darkness from taking over my life, once again.

So what could I do now? I had some choices laid out in front of me, but none of them felt particularly appealing. Complete and utter devastation, was a huge piece of this process for me. So was radical acceptance. I had learned to accept and to process so much trauma and deep seated pain. This healing journey had been nothing short of profound for me. So as I studied the choices laid out before me, I thought long and hard, about what I should do next; about what I COULD do next, to become UNSTUCK. All I knew, was that I missed the light. I missed the glorious light. Looking back on it now, I

201

think a lot of what pushed me back into the darkness, was the realization that my life was not going to be perfect, even after all of the healing work I had done, and was continuing to do. I mean, wasn't it enough that I had been abused in the first place? Wasn't it enough, that I had spent years of my life now, working incredibly hard to mend and to heal my shattered and torn up soul? It felt so unfair to me, that life couldn't be perfect. I thought that perfect was what I needed, to feel whole; to be able to handle my life. But I was wrong. I didn't need perfection. What I needed, was authenticity. I realized that I was still two separate people. Half of me was an adult, and the other half of me was still that seven year old little girl, with the sunken eyes, and the disappearing shape. I had spent all of this time healing; all of this time trying to fix her. Why wasn't she merged with me yet? After all that I had done for her, how could she still be triggered so deeply, by her trauma? I found myself getting very frustrated with her; with myself. I just wanted this process to be over. I didn't want to do this any-more. I didn't want to think about rape. I didn't want to talk about it. I didn't want to think about torture. I didn't want to torment myself any longer, by doing this work. I. WAS. DONE. I was ready to throw in the towel, call it day, get back in my bed, pull the covers over my head, and never come out again.

I think one of most important things that I learned in my healing process, was in this moment; during the darkest I had felt, since this whole thing had begun. I learned that sitting with your pain, can be a very powerful and liberating experi-ence. Whenever I had to sit with uncomfortable feelings, I would squirm around like a toddler with ADHD. I couldn't sit still. I felt like my head was going to explode. I felt like if I didn't keep myself moving, that I was going to crawl out of my skin. During this most difficult phase of my healing jour-ney, I made some really tough decisions. Ultimately, I chose the harder choice. The easier choice, would have been to quit; to simply give up, and tell my therapist that I was healed up enough for a lifetime, and that I was DONE talking about this shit, for lack of a better word. I am so incredibly thankful, that I found the strength and the bravery inside my soul, to keep at it; to keep going. I dug deep. I. DUG. DEEP. I told myself that I had come too far, to bow out now. Ali told me that I had worked too hard, and had come too far to give up. I didn't tell her that I was thinking about throwing in the towel. I didn't have to; she could see it written all over my face. I hated how well she knew me. These days, I take so much comfort in it; in being known. And so, I learned how to sit with my pain. I learned how to breathe through it. I learned how to soak in it, without getting swallowed up. I allowed it to sit so close to me. I allowed it to envelope me. And something amazing began to take place. I found that when I stopped fighting against it; that when I stopped fighting against feeling it and just allowed it to come, that it would wash over me like a storm, and leave me just as swiftly as it came. I remember thinking to myself, "this wasn't that bad. I can do this." Mastering the art of sitting in your pain but not getting stuck in it, is a huge part of the healing process. It is both excruciatingly painful at times, but necessary. It's all about finding balance. It's all about accepting that our lives are going to always have ups and downs, no matter what. And for me, finding that balance proved to be a far more difficult task, than I had anticipated. It's why I kept circling around to the same place, over and over and over again. It's why that little girl inside of me, was still screaming at the top of her lungs. It's why she was still triggered by her trauma, in a way that rendered her unable to "deal" with her life. During the darkest night of my soul, I uncovered my own strength. It is the place, where my resilience came to life. It is the place, where that little girl and I, had finally merged together as a whole person; beautifully broken, and put back together again. In that dark place, was where I

learned how to hold onto hope, for longer periods of time. In

that cold dark space, is where I learned how to balance and

steady myself, on uneven and shaky ground. It is the place,

where I became unbreakable. In the most unlikely place; in the

darkest of moments, I had discovered the power, of my own

light.

Little girl speak

"In case no one's told you lately, or ever: I'm so proud,

of all you've accomplished in your life, and I'm so proud of

who you are. I know we've had a rough go of things.

Life sure hasn't ever been gentle with us, or easy on us.

But you rose up like a lion, and you fought back.

You refused to let the darkness define you, or break you.

I'm so incredibly proud of you. No one I know deserves

happiness more than you. God knows you've worked so hard

for decades of your life, to grow through the concrete we got

slammed into over and over again, when life knocked us

down. Never forget, that there is beauty in how we fall.

Strength, in how we continue to breathe.

Courage, in how we decide to keep fighting.

And fierceness, in how we rise."

-Little girl speak

"Fierce warriors are always made, when the earth and the roots beneath them shake. And while nothing can stop this battle from taking place, you are made up of fire and water and light. And I know that you have what it takes."

-Little girl speak

Chapter 13

Finding your Fierce

Little girl speak

This phase of my healing process, was nothing short of a miracle. I had been trapped in a dark night of the soul, for what seemed like forever. Finally, I was clawing my way back up to the surface and out into the light again. Oh that glorious light. I remember sitting on my front porch, just soaking it in; just basking in the light of the warm sun shining down on my face. I felt its rays moving gently down my arms, all the way through to my fingertips. And for the very first time in my life, I felt deeply connected to the world around me. Not just present; but connected. I had spent my entire life, feeling so hopelessly tortured and alone. But now here I stood, feeling connected to everything and everyone around me. A neighbor passed by walking her dog. Another one, carrying his mail from the day before. I smiled and waved. Never underestimate the power, of every day moments; of every day things. I had been so consumed by grief and shame for so long, that I didn't notice LIFE, happening all around me. These little moments of life, were like tiny treasures to be collected, and I was partici-

pating in them. I knew that these little moments, were of great

significance. They were signs of life; my life. I was finally be-

ginning to connect with my world, and everything in it. Slow-

ly but surely, I was finally moving into a new phase; a new

space; one that I had never seen in myself before. Finally, I

was beginning to live. I refer to this phase of my healing, as

FINDING MY FIERCE. So what does finding your fierce,

look like? You're probably thinking, "lady, I really hope that

you don't expect me to rip my own heart wide open, and do all

of that healing work, just be present enough to sit on a front

porch and feel the sun on my face, and wave to my neigh-

bors." Of course not. Of course there is so much more to it

than just that. But as my little sister Lizzy once said: "never

despise meager beginnings." This was just a beginning; a

place to start. And if you're like me, and you spent decades of

your life so completely disconnected from your body and from the world around you, you will appreciate these little every

day moments, so much more than you could possibly imagine

right now in this moment. So what is, Finding your FIERCE?

It can be many things, from small seemingly insignificant vic-

tories, all the way up to life altering moments that you will

never forget. But it begins internally; it begins inside of you.

The only way to be present in all of your moments, is to first

connect with yourself; with your inner warrior; with your in-

ner FIERCE. How do you do that? What does it look like?

What does it feel like? As I mentioned earlier in this book, I

have received hundreds, probably thousands of messages from

survivors all over the world. Survivors who are in all different

stages of their healing journeys. The common chords that ran

through these messages, was a longing; this deep longing, to

forget. They wanted more than anything else, to forget what

happened to them. They asked me, if it was possible. They

begged me, to help them forget. My heart broke, as I read

these messages. Tears were streaming down my face, as I felt

every ounce of pain that they were pouring out onto the page. I

wanted so much, to be able to tell them YES; YES it IS possi-

ble to forget, and I can help you to do that. I did my best, to

comfort them. I did my best to respond in a way, that wouldn't

further break them. I tried to encourage them, that it wouldn't

always feel this way; that the pain wouldn't always feel this

intense. I tried to lift them up as best I could; to empower and

encourage them, to keep going. This chapter is probably the

most important one for me to write, because it changed every-

thing for me. And I'm hoping that when you get to this place

in your own healing process, that it will change everything for

you too. Finding your FIERCE, discovering your truth, seeing

your worth, and the desire to make a difference in the world

around you; all of these things, are inextricably connected. As

you begin to find your FIERCE, the rest will naturally fall into

place. Life will fall into its own new rhythm; your rhythm.

You will begin to step into your authenticity. And once you do, believe me warrior woman, you will never want to step out of it again. So let's talk about these four steps: finding your FIERCE, discovering your truth, seeing your worth, and the desire to make a difference in the world around you.

Finding your FIERCE

This is what finding your FIERCE, looks like. This is what finding your FIERCE, feels like. It is the acknowledgement that you are more than the sum of what's happened to you. It is the belief that you are more than just skin; more than just bones. It is recognizing that there is a strength inside you, that's been buried beneath your trauma. It is a commitment to yourself, to bring that strength to life. Here is what finding my FIERCE looked like, for me: hours spent meditating, just focusing on my breathing. You would be surprised, at how connecting with yourself in a quiet space, can awaken a warrior cry within you. At first, it's just a low and steady roar. And then it becomes louder and louder, like a battle cry; YOUR

battle cry. I spent time eating different types of foods. I had

starved myself for most of my life, so I didn't really know

what kinds of food I liked, or would enjoy eating. I went for

lots of nature walks. I went on hikes in the mountains. Find-

ing your FIERCE for me, was getting to know myself, on a

soul level. It was getting to experience who I was deep down,

without the trauma invading every waking moment of my

time, and my headspace. Finding my FIERCE was the feeling

of being comfortable and safe and at peace in my own skin for

the first time. I was finally coming into my own, and it felt

like coming home.

Discovering your truth

Discovering the truth of you who are and what you

love, can feel like a daunting task at first, but it can also feel

completely liberating and exhilarating. I felt like a kid in a

candy store. I was running around just looking at everything, trying to figure out what I wanted to try first. I discovered during this process, that I DON'T like skiing. I am AWFUL at it. WOAH, I mean AWFUL. I'm sure that people around me found me quite entertaining to watch, as I rolled down the hill instead of skiing down it, but that was the first and the LAST time, that I would EVER go skiing. I tried my hand at lots of things. Bowling, playing guitar, listening to different types of music. I know that these things are all external, but they helped me to learn some things about myself, that ran far beneath the surface. I discovered some truths about myself; about who I was on the inside. I discovered that I am very passionate; that I put one hundred percent of myself, into whatever I'm doing at any given moment. I discovered that I am patient. I had somehow learned to be more patient with myself. I guess it was a lesson that I had learned, during my healing process. I also spent some time doing really difficult things, like researching issues that the church had ingrained in my brain, were taboo. Things like homosexuality, and divorce. I spent several months researching these issues, and talking with scholars and therapists. It was interesting to hear about different points of view on these topics. The common thread was that each person felt very strongly about their opinion of what the truth was. They stood firm in their convictions, and I liked that; even those that I didn't agree with. I think it's so important to stand firm in your truth, once you figure out what it is. The only truth I had ever connected with in my life, was that I was "damaged goods." I felt like I had those words invisibly branded across my forehead like a scarlet letter, and that predators could always see it. This was the first time in my life, that I was figuring out what I liked to do. This was the first time in my life, that I was figuring out what I believed in, and what I felt was the truth, for me. And I was fiercely determined, to hold tightly to my newfound convictions. I want to encourage you, to try new things. Eat new foods. Go to

217

places you've never been before. Try new activities. Maybe take up painting or drawing. Maybe try learning how to play a musical instrument. If you're like me, and trauma had dominated most of your life up until this point, you won't really know yet, what you like and what you don't like. Go back and do some things that used to make your soul happy as a child. See if you still love doing those things. The most important thing about discovering your truth, is that it will propel you into the next step of your healing; it will propel you into the most important steps of all.

Seeing your worth

THIS. IS. EVERYTHING. If you take absolutely nothing else with you, when you close the pages of this book, (I hope you take more with you) THIS is what I want you to take away; THIS is what I want you to hold onto for dear life: YOU. ARE. WORTHY. If I look back and think about how many decades it took me to believe this truth about myself, it breaks my heart. It shatters my soul into a million tiny pieces. We as women in general, spend so much time thinking that we are undeserving and unworthy. Then when you throw trauma and abuse from early childhood into the mix? FORGET IT. I may as well have come out of the womb and crawled right back in, because it was the only place I ever felt safe and inherently worthy, in my entire life. No matter what stage of healing you are currently residing in; even if you haven't begun your healing process yet, know this truth from the depths of your soul. Speak this truth over and over again to yourself, even when you don't feel it; especially when you don't feel it. Speaking truth to yourself, is KEY. Those who abused you spoke lies to you, over and over again. Maybe you believed those lies instantly, or maybe you slowly began to believe those lies over time, and claim them as your truth. You can rerecord those negative tapes. You can change them into affirmations of love, and acceptance. I remember standing in front of my mirror one morning, telling myself that I was worthy. I mean I literally rolled my eyes, as the words came out of my mouth. It took me a long time to believe those words. It took a long time, of daily speaking that truth to myself over and over again, before it finally started to sink in; before I finally started to believe it. As you begin to find your FIERCE, and discover your own truth more and more, you will begin to see your worth, on a deeper and broader level. It's amazing how that happens; how one aspect of your healing, will have a domino effect on the rest. Finding your FIERCE, will lead to the desire to discover your truth. Discovering your truth, will lead to you to finally being able to see your worth. All of these separate pieces, when connected together, will lead to the most amazing puzzle piece of all.

The desire to make a difference in the world around you

This is it. This one is it. This is the most important thing that happened to me, during my entire healing journey.

Little girl speak

I can't pinpoint the exact moment when it happened, but it happened; of that much, I am certain. I became hyper aware of the world around me, but not in an aftermath of trauma sort of way; this was different. This was very different. I began to look at the world, through a new set of eyes. I felt like I had developed a super power; like I could read minds. I began to pay close attention to the facial expressions and the body language of others, and I was amazed at what I saw. One day when I was at the park with my son, I saw these two moms talking on a bench, while their children played together in the sandbox. I couldn't hear the content of their conversation, nor was I trying to eavesdrop. But I paid attention to their body language. They were both very animated as they spoke to each other. I heard a lot of laughter. I saw a lot of exchanged smiles between them, and eventually toward the end of the conversation, a hug. Then the one mom got up and walked over to the sandbox, gathered up her child and all of his toys, placed him in his stroller, and began to walk away toward the parking lot. When I glanced back at the other mom, who was still sitting there on the park bench, she didn't even look like the same person. Her entire demeanor had changed. She was slouching down now, almost falling off the bench. She had this pensive look on her face, and her leg began to shake back and forth, with what I presumed to be anxiety. I looked closely at her eyes. They were tired. She looked exhausted. She looked like she was about to cry right there in the middle of the park, on a sunny summer afternoon. My heart went out to her. I wanted to walk up and just hug her. I wanted to tell her, that she didn't have to pretend to be happy in front of her friend; that she didn't have to hide those more difficult pieces of herself, from the world. But I also didn't want to be THAT girl; the weird lady who walks up to strangers in the park and hugs them. Is there even such a person? Well if there was, it surely wasn't gonna be me. But I sat there for a while, hoping that her son

222

would begin to interact with mine. I was waiting, and hoping to have the opportunity to talk to her. Sure enough about five minutes later her little boy came over to my son, and plopped down in the sand next to him. My son has special needs, and he doesn't speak. This little boy couldn't have been more than two years old, and he was eager to wave to my son and say hi. They began sharing the shovels and playing with toys in the sand. The woman stood up and pushed her stroller over to my side of the sandbox, where our boys were now playing together. Then she sat down next to me on the park bench. "Hi." She said. "Hi." I said. "How old is your little boy?" She asked. "He's eight years old, but developmentally he's around one. He has down syndrome, autism, and juvenile diabetes, so life with this little guy is busy for sure." I said. "Wow." She said. "Bless your heart and bless him. That must be so difficult sometimes huh? I couldn't imagine. You're a very strong person." She said. "It's all relative." I said. "What do you mean?"

223

She said. "Pain." I said. "Challenges. Experiences that happen to us or around us, that shape who we are, what we do, and how we love. No one's experiences or challenges should be compared to another's, because we all have struggles. We all go through periods when life is just hard." She didn't say anything. "Oh great." I thought. I just got all philosophical and too personal with the mom I met at the park, and now she's gonna get up and awkwardly walk away from me, and leave me sitting here feeling like a complete idiot. But she didn't. The two of us just sat there, connecting. We talked about the difficulties of motherhood, and of being a wife and a homemaker. She told me how lonely she felt sometimes. I did my best to encourage her and lift her spirits. I asked her if I could give her a hug. We embraced, and then we gathered up our boys, and went our separate ways, toward home. I shook my head the entire ride. What had just taken place? What was that? How did that happen, and why? It was as if time had

224

stood still. Two strangers sat on a park bench, connecting

deeply for a brief moment in time. That conversation brought

me so much comfort, that I wasn't alone in my struggles. And

I'm sure it brought the same comfort to her. I could tell that

she had needed to connect with someone, and I was so hon-

ored that she opened up to me. It felt so natural to me, to draw

her out. I knew that helping people was what I wanted to do

most. I also believe that giving a person the freedom to feel

comfortable enough to be themselves, is incredibly important.

As I made myself my morning cup of coffee the next day, I

started thinking about the future. I was so excited that I was

even at the point in my journey, where I could do that. For so

long I had to live moment by moment, just to be able to make

it through the day. Now here I was a few years later, standing

in my kitchen with a hot cup of coffee in my hands, dreaming

about changing the world. I felt that little girl inside of me,

grinning from ear to ear. She was determined, to make a

difference. She was determined to take her pain, and turn it into something good, by helping others to heal. If she could do that, then all of her suffering was not for nothing; it was not in vain. She wasn't going to let it be in vain. She was determined to create a safe space for other survivors, where they could come, and be believed. A place where they could come and be known, and seen, and loved. I can't pinpoint the exact moment that it happened; but it happened. That little girl inside of me was no longer a victim; she was a survivor. She was a survivor on a mission, to change the world. And there I was, standing in my kitchen, hot cup of coffee in my hands, staring out the window with a smile on my face; so incredibly honored, that she was taking me along, for the ride.

So how was she going to do it? What platform would this determined little warrior inside of me use, in order to reach other survivors and make a difference? "Writing." I thought. Writing has to be it. I had been writing all my life. It seemed like the most natural choice for me. What about you?

I know it's probably really difficult to think that far ahead

right now, but you will get to this place on your own journey,

so be thinking of some things that you could do that would fill

your soul, and at the same time, help others around you. May-

be for you, it's volunteering somewhere. Maybe it's painting

and posting healing artwork on social media. The list is end-

less, of ways we can make a different in the world around us.

You will find your calling. You will find your niche, when the

time is right. I had found my niche. I knew exactly what I

needed to do. I needed to start a blog. I had written so many

quotes, poems, and spoken word pieces during my healing

journey. The thought of sharing them with the world, terrified

me in the beginning. But I gave myself some time to get used

to the idea, before actually doing it. I gave myself the rest of

that summer and the fall season, to mentally and emotionally

prepare for this advocacy work that I was about to do. I gave myself some time, to get used to this newly found freedom

that I was living in. I gave myself some time to just breathe,

and prepare. I did a lot of research online, and Facebook

seemed to be the best platform for what I was looking to do. I

finally launched my Facebook blog page: *Little girl speak,* on

January 9th of 2018. I shared different things that I had writ-

ten, and some things from other writers and bloggers as well.

There were days in the beginning, when I ached from the

sheer vulnerability of it all. But as time went on, it got easier

and easier, to share my heart; to share my struggles and my

triumphs, with the world. The most important thing that I

wanted other survivors to know, is that they are not alone.

They are not walking alone, in their quest for healing. I want-

ed them to know, that they are so deeply loved. I did my best

to create a safe place, where survivors can come and gain sup-

port; where they can be understood and validated in their feel-

ings, and where they can be nurtured and loved, and ultimately empowered and inspired to find their voice again; to find the courage to keep going; to keep fighting; to keep healing. I never expected the growth that would happen, from the moment I launched *Little girl speak*. There I was, just six months later since launch, with over 20,000 followers. I was receiving hundreds of messages a week, asking me about what my healing process looked like. I knew that this book needed to come next; and so I slowly began writing it. At the one year mark since the launch of my blog, I was at over 37,000 followers and growing. On one hand, it broke my heart to know how many survivors existed; that there are so many of us; that there are so many lives affected by this horrific type of pain. But on the other hand, it gave me comfort. Comfort that I am not alone. Comfort that I'm making a difference; that I might be providing the only safe place that someone might have right now, to come and get support. I take the responsibility of my blog very seriously. I do my best to wake up every day, and bleed truth from my soul, in the form of ink on a page. I use quotes and poems and pieces on my blog, that I wrote throughout the course of my healing journey. I have also written a lot of new pieces, since the launch of my blog. It is an honor and a privilege every single day, to do this advocacy work; to interact with the bravest and most courageous souls, on the planet. I have received at this point, probably thousands of messages from survivors all over the world, thanking me for my blog. Thanking me for being brave enough to speak my truth, and to say the words that they themselves have not been able to find, or haven't felt strong enough to say yet. I am amazed and in awe, every time I read these messages. That spunky little girl inside of me, IS changing the world. She is making a difference in the lives of other survivors, and I couldn't be more proud of her. That blog isn't just a safe place for other survivors; it's a safe place for her too; for me. It's a community; a family. It is an army of fierce survivors; of warrior women, who finally refuse to back down; who finally refuse to be silent.

So you see how it all ties together? It starts inside you, by finding the strength that's buried within, discovering the truths of what you believe, seeing the worth of who you are, and figuring out how you can make a difference in the world; how you can make a difference, in the lives of those who cross your path. It all starts with your healing. Your healing will not only be the greatest gift you've ever given yourself; it will also be the best gift that you could possibly give, to the world. The world needs you to be YOU. Uniquely YOU. The world needs your gifts. The world needs you to do the things that make your soul come alive. In finding what those things are and in being healed up enough to do them, you will make this world a brighter place and a better place, for all of us; yourself included. So hold onto hope, Little One. If I can come to this point in my journey, then so will you. This healing is yours for the taking. All you have to do, is reach out and grab ahold of it. Take it in your hands, and cradle it. Fall in love with the idea, of mending your soul. And don't be afraid of the darkness. It won't last forever, I promise. You will come out on the other side of it; stronger, more grounded, and whole.

Little girl speak

"Don't you dare lose sight of that magic inside you.

You have walked through fire, and a thousand hurricanes.

You survived all the things that tried so hard to break you.

You allowed all the pain, to sink in so deeply.

Though it no longer defines you, you couldn't stay the same.

Keep speaking your truth out loud.

This world, is gonna know your name.

Look how you allowed that fire, to refine you.

Gorgeous woman, you have been remade."

-Little girl speak

"You have the strength deep inside you. Your soul knows exactly what it has to do. The world is waiting, for you to make history. We're all patiently waiting, for you to bloom."

-Little girl speak

Chapter 14

All grown up

Little girl speak

It's not easy being a grownup; especially not one who had to FIGHT, to grow up. So here she was; that little girl inside of me, all grown up. I was becoming more and more proud of her, every day. I watched her fight battles effortlessly, that used to bring her to her knees. I stood in awe and amazement, of what this process had done for her; of what it had done for me. This is the phase of my healing journey where I probably learned the most about what it means, to regulate your emotions, and to balance yourself in the real world; in the everyday happenings of life; in the chaos of it all. Balance and boundaries. Those are the two words that came to define my life, and bring order to my world. And don't think for a moment, that I was perfect at this. Oh no. No no no. Like every other stage of my healing process, I struggled. I went through my normal phases of denial, self-awareness and eventually, acceptance and love. I began to notice some patterns in myself, that were different; good patterns.

Little girl speak

Patterns like allowing myself to feel hurt over things, but not allowing it to dominate my day. Patterns like being able to offer myself grace when I made a mistake, instead of beating myself up for hours over it. Patterns like being able to process triggers as they came up, without falling back into a black hole inside myself. I was doing it; I was regulating my emotions. And then, there were the boundaries. Oh that pesky little word. It is so important, to figure out what your boundaries are, and to enforce them. Boundaries are so healthy, for everyone. We all need them. They are what provide order and safety, in an otherwise completely chaotic world. I had never really had to set up boundaries in my life. I was always good at treating others with respect and dignity, but when it came to myself, I was a complete pushover. From the time that I was abused; maybe even before, I was a people pleaser. I never wanted to step on anyone's toes. I never wanted to hurt anyone's feelings. By this point in my healing process, I knew

what my boundaries needed to me, but I also knew that I was
going to have a difficult time setting them, and holding stead-
fastly to them. But here's the thing; here's the truth of it: the
only people, who will have an issue with you setting boundaries, are the ones who have continuously crossed them. SET
BOUNDARIES. Figure out what they are for you, and hold
tightly to them. Don't be afraid, to rock the boat. When it
comes to the issue of boundaries, don't be afraid of other people's hurt feelings; be more afraid, of your own. You have the
right as a human being, to set up boundaries that make you
feel safe. Physical boundaries. Emotional boundaries. The
more you progress in your healing process, the more you will
discover what boundaries make you feel at peace. And it is my
hope that you will begin to stand firm in those convictions.
Certain people in my life really tried to test my boundaries. I
felt like I should have listed them out on a three by five card,
and given them to people as gifts. (laughs out loud) I'm sure

my friends and family would have gotten a big kick out of that. But honestly, those boundaries became very important to me. It was about the knowledge, that I was finally listening to myself; that I was finally treating myself with respect, and giving myself what I needed, to feel safe in my world.

Let's go back to talking about balance, because I think that that's what most of life is; balancing things. We have to balance our work with our family. We have to balance our down time with our friend time. We have to balance what we eat. We have to balance the amount of time we spend exercising, watching TV, perhaps playing games on our iPad if that's applicable to you. (I am not a gamer type person) But seriously, think about it. Mostly everything we do in our lives, requires balance. For most adults, who were victims of childhood sexual abuse, balance is just not something that comes naturally or easily. We were forced to live in a constant state of fear and panic. Our hearts were always racing. Our minds

239

were always going a mile a minute. We had no way to process what was happening to us, or regulate our feelings about it, and so balance and order disappeared; it vanished. It went right out the window with the other things we needed, but didn't have; things like love, safety, nurturing, guidance, support. We were like little ships stranded at sea, with no coastguard in sight. Or worse; for some of us the coastguard came, and drowned us all over again. Trying to find balance in your life as a human being, is difficult enough. Trying to find balance as a survivor, is damn near impossible. But I was resolute in my desire to find it; to cultivate it; to live it. It took some time, but eventually I got pretty good at maintaining balance in my life. Regulating my emotions was a whole different story. During my healing process, my emotions were all over the place. That is to be expected. This is skill that you will pick up along the way, very slowly. Please be gentle with yourself, as you learn to regulate your emotions. I know we've talked about this a lot, in terms of the getting stuck vs staying stuck piece of things. All of that stuff is related to emotional regulation. Towards the beginning of my healing process, it was almost impossible to keep myself even keeled. But now? I was doing much better. I was able to process triggers more quickly, and without getting sucked into an abyss of anxiety and depression. I was learning how to sit with really uncomfortable feelings without running from them, but also not allowing them to dominate my mind, or take over my world. It was amazing; and it still is. I was finally able to handle my life and my stressors, in much healthier ways. I was finally relating and reacting to my world, as an adult; and not as a scared little girl who was frozen in time. Cultivating these skills of being able to balance your emotions, and hold tightly to your boundaries, will further propel you into the things that make your soul happy. And that is the best feeling of all.

This process of inner child healing, is a very difficult

road to walk. It is a very painful and grueling process. But look at all the beauty that you find along the way! Look at all the things you learn about yourself, and about the world around you! I know it's so hard right now; I know it's so incredibly painful, to endure this process; to suffer through the darkness. But this pain that you're feeling; it can't compare with the freedom and the joy that you will feel, on the other side of it. I have seen both sides now and trust me, it's like living in two different worlds. Your healing has to be intentional. I wish that I could go through this process for you, but I can't. It is my hope and my prayer, that you will be able to use this book as some type of framework, on your own journey. It is my hope that you come back to these pages when you need them, and that they will remind you that you are strong, and that you can do this, and that you are not alone. I stand with you, in these pages. I fight alongside you, in your quest for freedom. You already survived the abuse; so believe me brave warrior soul, you are strong enough to survive the healing. Please make the journey. Please make the choice, to embark on this path toward healing. It will be the best decision you've ever made. You won't regret it, I promise. You can move beyond surviving, into thriving. There is so much life left, on the other side of it. There is so much joy and hope, just waiting to be experienced. There is more to this life, than survival. Little One, there is so much more. Tap into the strength, that's buried inside you. You've already won the battle; now it's time, to win the war.

Little girl speak

"I am ever changing and rearranging these broken pieces you made. But I'm still beautiful as I'm breaking. I am history in the making. For I keep rising up, unafraid."

-Little girl speak

Chapter 15

Writings from my Journal

The rest of the pages in this book, are spoken word pieces and poems that I wrote in my journal, throughout my healing process. I wanted to share them with you, in the hopes that they will empower and inspire you, to keep fighting. I have selected pieces that honor every stage of this journey, from darkness into light.

"What are opinions, and why do we have them? What is the point, if we're not allowed to share them? What does it feel like to stuff them all down; to know that your words are so clearly viewed, as nothing more than chatter? It's like you're choking on every breath; fighting so hard to believe that you matter. How can you explain this feeling, to another? What it feels like, when your words are kept silent and violently smothered? Sometimes you just want to raise your voice, and scream. Sometimes that's all that's left, of what's been broken at the seams. You were never allowed to be a kid; not for one moment; not one second of it. You learned to suffer in silence; no one hearing your screams; no one seeing the sadness, that was neatly tucked behind your tired eyes. Nobody seeing you clenching your fists in anger, as you cried yourself to sleep, almost every single night. How can you explain what this feels like; why such rejection cuts so deep into your bones? How can anyone ever understand what it feels like, to be alive inside the body of a ghost? When you've walked alone your entire life, its damn near impossible, to let anyone see inside. You don't want them to see the holes; to see these gaping cracks. You don't want them to know your secrets; to see the emotional maturity that you lack. How can you learn to grow yourself up, when you're already fully grown? How can you survive with the mind of a child, when you're 36 years old? My innocence wasn't just stolen; it was ripped right out of me, and shattered completely wide open. A part of me will always be that seven-year-old little girl; the one who stared into her mirror, and hated her body instead of hating her world. The one who always takes the blame; the one who always owns all the shame. Most of me is trapped, in the desperate in-between. In the struggle, to find what is worth being spoken about; in the struggle, to fight not to purge, starve, or bleed. My mind is often similar, to the mind of a broken teenager. And all I want, is for her to find a way to grow up. To believe, that she is worthy of everything; to believe, that she is enough. She doesn't feel worthy of happiness. How could she possibly, after all of this? Her entire life, she's been drenched with pain. The scars of her survival just spinning in a circle, much like a weather vane. The only way out of this, is for her to feel every ounce of this pain. She wants to grow older, inside of her brain. She wants to move forward; far beyond the confines, of this collapsing space. How can you describe this chaos inside, to another human being? This fight to hold onto the heart that you built; when you were the only one who cared, if it kept on beating? Letting go and growing up inside, means admitting that you were wrong, in the ways you chose to survive. How can I tell that little girl, that her choices screwed up my life? She's already been abused, and rejected. How can I add to the shame and the blame, that she already feels, deep inside? How can I tell that teenage girl, that it's time for her to grow up? When she was never allowed, to have a voice; when she was always told, that she was never enough? But I guess this isn't about taking away; it's about finally stepping up to the plate. It's about learning how to balance the joy, and the pain. And learning the art, of not continuing to hold onto anyone else's shame. It's about learning when and what to share. It's about knowing who is safe, and who will stay and sit with you there. There is no shame in how I survived; it got me here to this place and time. These scars that I hold; I can claim them as mine. It's ok to own them; it won't break me inside. It's ok to feel the weight of this; the weight of this pissed off miserable kid. This teenager who had no voice, and the little girl who had no choice. All of this pain is heavily weighted. But starving my body, and cutting my skin, won't make it go away. It just leaves me there, sedated. Those choices won't remove this shame; they cannot alter, or change this pain. It's time for me to make new choices; to forge a new path. And I know, that I am fully capable. I don't have to remain that voiceless child,

247

because I am no longer invisible. I am no longer bound, to my past."

-Little girl speak

Little girl speak

Mirror

She's screaming so loud
I can hear her now.
She's biting that stuffed koala bear,
To muffle and drown out the sounds.
Her tiny body; penetrated.
Every ounce of her enraged,
By all of this terror,
Powerlessness and shame.
So much has changed
Inside of her over the years.
But when I hear her screaming,
It still reduces me to tears.
I want to reach out,
And grab hold of her,
And love her;
Pull her safely into my arms.
I want to rescue and restore her.
She fought so hard,
But she couldn't save herself.
And the pain transformed her
Into somebody else.
She spent her life surviving;
Never understanding
How to live.
She knew no way of thriving;
She had nothing left to give.
And when these nightmares
Swiftly come,
There's no place left
For me to run.
It's just me

cont...

Little girl speak

And my nightmares,
And all of this pain.
The feelings and memories
I cannot erase.
I cannot avoid them;
Each moment, vividly clearer.
No more starving it away,
Or purging it out;
No more turning it all on myself,
In the mirror.
So here I sit,
On my bedroom floor;
Just as I did,
All those decades before.
I am sitting once again,
In front of this piece of glass;
Holding onto different questions,
Than the ones I used to ask.
I used to sit in this very position;
Arms hugging my knees so tight.
And I would tell myself:
"You will make it; you will make it;
Just take a deep breath.
You will survive it again tonight."
But little girls
Shouldn't carry such things.
They shouldn't have to worry,
About anything.
I sat in front of that bedroom mirror,
Afraid, and without a safe home.
And it didn't matter which house I was in,
Because I always felt alone.
It was just me and my secrets,

cont...

Little girl speak

And my ability to keep them hidden,
And this innate obsession
With protecting everyone from them.
I did what I thought I needed to do,
But I had no idea
What would happen to me
After years and years,
Of not facing that abuse.
I've worked so hard
To recover from this;
To move beyond the weight of it.
But when I am triggered,
And these nightmares come,
I'm still so afraid,
And there's nowhere left to run.
And so here I sit,
In front of my mirror.
Arms hugging knees,
With visions grow clearer.
And I stare at myself;
At this woman's frame and shape;
At all of her scars,
That cannot be erased.
Frantically searching,
For that scared little girl.
I can still hear her,
But I can't seem to find her,
No matter how hard I try.
But as I slow down
And I take a deep breath,
I look up and there she is,
With those piercing
Dark brown eyes.

cont...

251

Little girl speak

Behind those eyes,
Is where she'll always be;
For she doesn't see the world
Like me.
She wasn't very happy.
And I have to stop
Expecting her to be.
She is allowed
To cry out,
When she is triggered.
She is allowed to break down,
When these memories come.
It is not my job
To silence her pain.
It's my job
To make her feel safe, and loved.
And somehow,
That has to be enough.
All I can give her,
Is the love
She deserved to have.
I've had to learn
To be her guardian;
To be the mother
She never had.
So here we sit, together;
Her big piercing eyes,
Inside my woman's frame.
And I remind her
That she's safe,
And that things
Are vastly different;
Even though

cont...

Little girl speak

In this moment,
They still feel the same.
I breathe in deeply
And I let it out slowly,
As I press my forehead
Against the glass.
And we sit here together,
Exhausted and weathered,
As we wait for these feelings
To pass.

-Little girl speak

Little girl speak

How Much?

"How much is a little girl worth? It is a question I've had to ask myself, far too many times. So tell me please. What is the answer? What is a little girl worth? What is her safety worth? What is her smile worth? What is her laughter worth? What is her childhood worth? What is her innocence worth? What is her life worth? Can you measure it, in dollars? Go ahead and pick a figure, and lay it all out here for me, on the table. In dollars and cents; what is she worth? How much should it cost to abuse and destroy her? She's just a little girl. She knows nothing, of dollars and cents. She only knows about fear; about being terrified, inside her own skin. She only knows about nightmares; about isolation and loneliness. She only knows about trust being broken; about hiding shameful secrets. She only knows about hating her body, and wanting so much; so desperately, to do anything to alter or change it. You can try to explain to her what you think her pain should be worth, but she won't understand it. For money is something, she hasn't yet earned. Her account doesn't hold dollars, but it holds many other things; like every memory of when she's laughed, and every song that she's ever learned to sing. Like all of the summers spent playing in the yard, and riding her bike in the sun. But slowly those memories have been replaced, by hauntingly darker ones. Her account has been depleted; everything's been stolen from her. All of the good has been emptied out. And that reality is really beginning to sting. She doesn't understand how you could put a price tag, on the happiness and the innocence, of another human being. The nightmare that you forced her to live. The grave that you pushed her into, and buried her alive in, she is using that pain; the worst part of her story, to help other souls; to save them. She is using her pain as a bridge; as a rope, to go back and to rescue each one of them. You picked the wrong little girl to

254

exploit. You put a price tag on her silence, but she grew up, and in spite of you, she still found her voice. You tried so hard to bury her, underneath the weight of all your shame. But she defeated you. She climbed out of the rubble, piece by piece. And a warrior, is exactly what she became. You cannot put a price tag, on what this freedom has cost her. She lost herself so many times, for those who didn't want her. For those, who chose not to protect her. But as she stands on this mountain top; her hands reaching down, to pull them all up; she realizes now, that she deserved every ounce of the love you never gave her; that she deserved every ounce of energy that you wasted, in exploiting and abusing her. And she didn't climb this mountain for you. She realizes now, that she did it for herself. She did it, to prove that these mountains could be moved. She did it, to inspire other survivors, like herself. She scaled these mountains; tall and wide, with pigtails in her hair. With gushing wounds, and gaping holes; with no one around her, who cared. So don't you dare take credit, for this warrior she's become. You had absolutely nothing to do with it. You never offered her an ounce of support, or love. She doesn't owe you an ounce of credit. Because she was alone, when push came to shove. So I will ask you again: what is a little girl worth? You won't answer the question, will you? It's because you know the truth; it's because her life is worth more to everyone else, than it has ever been worth, to you. But It's ok. I don't need you to answer the question. There is no answer you could give me, that would make this feel better. There's no answer on the planet, that could take away the sting. But as a mother myself, I stand here now before you. And I can tell you that the answer to my question, is: ABSOLUTELY EVERYTHING."

-Little girl speak

255

Little girl speak

Worthy

"She was determined. At the meager age of only six, she stood there on the precipice, of endless possibilities. The world she knew, was gracious and kind; filled with only love, and good things. She would lye awake in her bed at night, daydreaming about who she would become. Her future seemed so clear; so vividly bright. She felt wanted, seen, safe, and loved. But everything changed, at the age of seven. Her innocence collided, with the darkest of demons. Years of her life, were ripped from her hands; in a moment; in an instant. And she learned very quickly, how to fake a smile; how to play pretend. She learned to keep existing, long after her life had come to an end. She wrestled with a piece of glass, for years to come. She stood there, in front of its smudge stained surface; wondering if she could ever truly be loved. Something horrific happens, when little girls are penetrated. They see the world as a scary, and unsafe place. They see themselves as damaged goods. They internalize their rage. It morphs, into the worst form, of self hate. She starved herself of every good thing. She only gave herself the crumbs. She equated the food, with shamefulness; and the tiny morsels that she allowed herself to consume, was the amount of love she felt worthy of. If I could go back and let her speak; if I had not silenced her painful screams; if I had been brave enough, to believe that I was worthy. What could have become of me? Would I be different? Would my heart, not have these gaping holes in It? Would I not die inside, every time I hear the word RAPE? Would my level of empathy and compassion have changed? Who would I be, if he had never raped me? This question has haunted me, for so many years. I have tried for decades, to find the answer; to put back together those childhood moments; the ones that were dominated by loneliness, terror, and unimaginable fear. But the problem doesn't lie within the answers; it lurks among the

questions. The things she asked herself for years, were mis-
guided misdirections. The question is not was she worthy of
love; but rather, why did she not believe that she was? The
question was not why did he rape her, but rather why did she
turn it on herself in the mirror? These are the questions, that
make warriors even braver. I was brave enough to face my
demons, and I am strong enough, to trample and defeat them.
My journey has been long; an endless quest to heal. But what
it truly comes down to, is learning how to feel. It's learning
how to not shut down. It' learning how to let the pain come; to
feel it; to touch it; and to know in the midst of it, that I was
NEVER unworthy, of love."

-Little girl speak

Little girl speak

Forget

"How is a little girl, ever supposed to come back from that kind of a hell? How can she survive, when she is reminded every day of her torture? It plays over and over again, inside my mind. It's long since been over, but on days like today, my body can't seem to tell. My hands and my knees start shaking, and my heart starts pounding. My body gets stiff, and still. I never feel put back together again. Something deep inside of me still feels so dirty. I'm so scared, that it always will. I don't know if I still believe anymore, that I can be made fully whole. I'm scared that if I let myself dwell on these feelings, that maybe I might lose control. I was seven years old. I never had a choice. So don't you dare stand there in silence, and stare at me blankly. Don't you tell me, that BOYS WILL BE BOYS. This man raped me over and over again, and he's the one who gets to be free, while I live like a prisoner, with his demons in my head. I will never forget what he did to me. I will never be the same again. I've spent my whole life, trying to escape from this pain; trying so incredibly hard, to forget.

-Little girl speak

Little girl speak

Invisible

"Do you ever feel invisible; like no one could see you, even if you wanted them to? Do you ever feel powerless; like no matter how many good things you do, that it all hinges on a self-worth, that shows up empty and non-existent? Do you ever feel broken; unable to process these feelings unspoken? This pain that runs like a constant chord, as it rips right through your chest. And try as you may, you can't seem to move forward. Even when you've given it all that you've got; even when you've shown up; armor on, and did your best? Do you ever feel like it's all pointless; the waking and sleeping; the working and breathing? Do you ever feel your anxiety rising to the point, where your mind becomes unhinged, from your body? Do you ever feel like the more you do, the less that you become? Do you ever wonder what it would feel like, to be wholly and deeply loved? How can I love a body, that's been mangled up and used? How can I love a mind, that's been manipulated and abused? How can I be present in thought, and feel the weight, of what's beneath? How can I see past this river of pain that flows through the core of me? It's in every crevice of my body. It's in every ounce of my aching bones. It settled itself in-between every crack. It filled in all the holes, and in those spaces, made its home. This pain is like a darkness, that swallows all the light. It lays dormant sometimes when the sun comes out, but it always reappears in time. It never fully leaves me alone, and I can't seem to figure out why. It's the source behind this madness I feel. It's inside every tear, that falls from my eyes. They escape my body, in shouts and screams; these demons, that don't ever seem to leave. They just lay there with my body; completely intertwined, and I've done everything I can do, to rid myself of them. I've tried so hard, to leave them behind."

-Little girl speak

Little girl speak

"I have to keep so many things compartmentalized. I have so
many boxes inside of my mind. And these boxes can never
touch. They can never collide. For the moment that they do,
my rage will hit the outside. Shutting down and numbing out.
Denying my fears, and all my doubts. Hiding this pain from
the inside out. Blood is screeching within my veins. Counting
the scars, within my remains. Skeleton eyes. So empty and
afraid, as I stare at the mess, that this chaos has made. Choices
not given, as my voice was taken. They grabbed it, and stole it
from me. They locked it inside me in a place so deep, that
even I, cannot find the key. Help me. Fix me. Somebody
please, come and save me from myself. All I hear inside my
head, is the sound of her screaming. All I see when I look in
the mirror, is the shadow of someone else. This pissed off
child inside of me, is waging a war within my bones. She's
sucking me dry with her anger and her sadness, wreaking havoc wherever she goes. I'm not powerless to stop her, but I just
don't think it's fair. Not one soul had come to save her. There
was never anybody there. Just her and the monster, and her
own nightmares. He gave them to her, to hold onto for him.
He ruined her existence, and he didn't even care. She just
wants it to be over. It's never really over. No matter how
many times, she works through the pain. She fights this feeling of shame, deep inside her. It's attached itself to her name.
Please, somebody come and save her. Her soul is so tired, and
afraid. All she wants, is to leave this damage behind her.
These wounds, that his hands have made. Can someone please
remind her, that she is still a warrior; that it's ok for her to cry;
that she will move on from this space? Right now, there is
nothing but doubt that surrounds her. She doesn't want to take
this pain, to her grave."

-Little girl speak

Little girl speak

Cut

"I'm down. Woman down. I'm cut, like the branch of a tree. Split off, from the rest of myself. Sliced open at the knees. I'm unable to move. I'm unable to breathe. All I can smell is the burning of flesh, as my bones are protruding from me. And all of those dreams I'd been hoping for, lay in scattered pieces, here on the floor. I find it best not to dream anymore. Life has a way of punching me in the face every time; of trying to even out the score. I search for my roots. They are nowhere to be seen. I was cut down and tossed away, as I bleed. It's hard to build a home out of rubble. I'd rather build a wall; even one that could cave in. I can hope to God, that they buy into the illusion and not try to scale it, because it's not about keeping them out; it's about protecting what's left within. This heart of mine, has been worn paper thin. It wasn't built to withstand such pressure. It wasn't built, to handle the weight of their sins. Far too many hands have touched this body, in places they shouldn't have been. And there's no time left to compartmentalize it all. I've been burned alive, from the outside in. I'm sitting here buried in this pile of ashes, with nothing left of me. The only way out, is to rebuild myself again; to claw my way to the surface, and regain my ability to dream. At the core of me I am very strong; so much braver than I believe. I have to find a way, to tear down this wall; to allow myself to be seen. I can't go back to those winding roots. I can't change where I came from, but I don't have to stay. It's time for me to be replanted someplace else. It's time to gather my heart, and what's left of my hope; turn around, and walk away."

-Little girl speak

Little girl speak

War

"And I have leaned to make far too much sense, out of tragedies. I have justified all of the darkness you held, but I cannot
wrap my mind around what it all means. What does the cold
hard truth, say about me? Am I nothing more than a pushover?
Nothing more than the bones of a frail little girl, who's lived
her whole life afraid? At the end of the day, are these wounds
that I've self inflicted, any better or worse than the wounds
you have made? And what can be said of our story? I never
wanted your history to be entangled with mine. I will forever
bear the weight of these things that you've done to me. I will
carry this damage, for the rest of my life. Most days it feels
like I'm drowning; like someone keeps shoving my head under water, expecting that I can keep breathing. I push myself
harder and harder to swim; to not reach out for help; to not get
lost in the nothingness. Some days it feels like I'm flounder-
ing; like I'm out here all alone. No safe place to plant my feet
on the ground; no place to call my home. A vagabond, with
walls so paper thin. A prisoner of a war, that never should
have been. You raped the soul of a seven year old girl. You
snuffed out her innocence; you obliterated her world. And you
get to be free, while she's still here drowning; while she's
gasping for air, as she fights to keep breathing. Some days her
heart has to fight so damn hard, in order to just keep beating.
You got all the freedom. No fear of the dark; no sleepless
nights. You abused and you raped, in this war that you waged;
and she'll be fighting your darkness, for the rest of her life."

-Little girl speak

Little girl speak

Sometimes

"Sometimes, I dream about you. I awake, to find myself screaming; heart pounding, hands sweating; my entire body shaking. I have to talk myself down; back into the reality of where I am sitting. Back into a world, where I sort of belong. This place, where I've managed to squeeze myself into, as I still search to find the meaning. I long to take up less space in the world. It's something that I've struggled with, since I was just a little girl. Thinner and thinner. Smaller and smaller. But the less I became, my pain just grew taller. My need to speak out, became stronger and stronger. How did you learn, how to do it so well; to silence little girls, and drag their souls to hell? I've been battling your demons, for practically my entire life. You gave me these things, that were never meant to be mine. And I'm still sitting here silent, just holding it all inside. Like a scared little girl. Like a gullible child. When I look in the mirror, I don't want to see myself. There are days I would give almost anything, to be anybody else. This skin of mine is thin and small. Sometimes I don't feel safe, inside of its walls. Never protected. She was never protected. And you can't imagine the weight, of having to live with that rejection. It sent her down a path, of introspection. Decades of her life spent hating herself, consumed by self degradation. The roots. The roots. They told her, it all comes back to the roots. But what do you do, when the roots are all bad? When the only people who showed you any affection, were the same people who let you get raped, again and again? Other little girls would tell me stories about princesses, and about fictional monsters who lived under the bed. But I knew nothing of fairytales. I only knew of these nightmares, every time I laid down my head. I knew absolutely nothing of fictional creatures, who hid underneath my bed. I only knew of the truth. And I thought those girls to be foolish, but I still wished that I was one of them.

263

Little girl speak

Because the truth, is that monsters are
very real, and they don't live under beds. They find a way, to
hide in plain sight; inside the bodies, of trusted grown men."

-Little girl speak

Little girl speak

Tornado

There is this calm,
Before the madness begins.
An eerie feeling that creeps,
From underneath the skin.
You look up and you see it;
This mighty whirlwind.
You stand there beneath it,
And wait for it to begin.
You close your eyes,
But it won't disappear.
Just because you choose
Not to see it anymore,
Doesn't mean that it isn't still here.
It touches down,
In perfect harmony
With the sky.
It spreads across the roads before it,
Leaving destruction all around it.
It claims the darkness,
And possesses the light.
Everything it touches,
Is whisked away.
It's dropped back down,
In a different time and place.
And before You have a chance
To catch your breath;
Up, up you go;
You're taken up
Inside of it.
You can hear them all screaming,
From down below.

cont...

Little girl speak

Some are running,
Some are paralyzed,
And some,
Won't let any emotion
Come or go.
They're all so different
In their reactions;
In the way
That they handle
The storm.
Some cower beneath
The branch of a tree,
And some go after it,
As if they're seeking more.
Their cries become blurred,
As you move further away.
You center yourself
In the eye of the Tornado,
And this is where you decide
You will stay.
It's somehow peaceful here;
Somehow comforting.
You find solace
In the darkness
That surrounds you.
You find hope
In the emptiness,
Of owning nothing.
Everything is gone;
Everything you once owned.
You have no place
To go back to.
You no longer

cont...

Little girl speak

Have a home.
It's all just a pile of rubble,
Staring blankly from the ground.
The storm took everything you had,
Without a moment's notice.
It whisked you away,
Without a sound.
This is where you live now;
Inside this storm.
You get used to the madness,
And the way that the wind
Flails you about,
And whips you around.
But you never get used to
The noise that it makes,
Every time it touches down.
And where is it taking you?
There's just no way of knowing.
It feels so damp and cold
Inside this space where you are.
You take a deep breath
And hope for the best.
After all, you're still alive;
You've made it this far.
You close your eyes again,
Disillusioned at your core.
And all of a sudden,
You know that it's over;
There is ground
Beneath your feet,
Once more.
But nothing is as it should be,
Even though the storm

cont...

Little girl speak

Has gone away.
Nothing looks like it did before;
Nothing is the same.
I opened my eyes
To empty spaces,
Where warmth and hope
Used to dwell.
I looked around
At the sheer devastation,
And suddenly
I didn't feel so well.
There is nothing
But calamity;
Just shattered pieces,
Of what happiness
Used to look like;
Of what holding onto hope
Used to feel like.
Everything is just a fragment;
Just an empty shell,
Of what it used to be.
And the worst part is,
That I've realized the truth.
I am not inside the tornado;
I never really was.
For it, was inside
Of me…

-Little girl speak

Little girl speak

Joy

"Joy. Such an elusive concept, for a girl like me. I've spent my entire life chasing after it. Or maybe just maybe, it's been chasing after me. One taste of it, and I become undone. I have always been deathly afraid of it. It's never made a home, of my bones. It doesn't know what to do with my pain. It cannot process my story. My efforts to hold onto it, have all been in vain. I've conquered entire wars, without possessing its glory. The slightest thought of perceived joy, sends shivers down my spine. It's like I'm living in a backwards universe; forever trapped, and suspended in time. And oh how I wish to God I could tell you, that I don't know the reasons why. But they play over and over inside of my head, like an upside down fairytale rhyme. Those of us who were prisoners, who have forcibly lived at the edge of hell; when we hear the sound of hope, it doesn't sit quite so well. It has been woven into our dreams, that hope is not meant to be held. We grew up in a place, where we were just bodies without a face. Deep inside, we were caged in a cell. Hell is where I lived. And hell is all that I knew. I never had control over anything in my life. I did what I was told to do. Joy simply did not exist in my world. I never really knew what it felt like, to be a carefree little girl. I held the weight of the world, on my tiny little shoulders. My body began to change as I grew, but my mind wasn't getting older. And no sentences I can manage to string together, will ever be able to describe how that really felt. I wanted him to kill me. I wanted so badly, to die. I wished every day, that I could switch lives with someone else. I didn't want to be that scared little girl. I didn't want to be myself. He made me so terrified; so afraid of the world. So scared, that I stuffed all my joy deep inside. I buried it alive, on some dusty worn out shelf. The day that hope finally found me, I was crushed, but unafraid. I had found the strength and bravery to speak of it out loud; all those horrible wounds, that he made. This healing process, is cyclical. It is two steps forward, and one step back at best. You sort of learn how to wear all the damage; how to deal with whatever's still left. I had given up on joy, until it found me once again; until I came to realize, this cycle I was in. It isn't abnormal. It's just the way that it is. You will recycle this pain; over and over again. But every time you do, its weight will become a little bit lighter. You will find a peaceful space; a fierce warrior within yourself. And you'll begin to learn how and where to find her. Your healing will never be linear. It's always an uphill climb. But you will find treasures along the way; ones that are sure to stand the test of time. You will find your voice again. You will find the courage to speak. You will find yourself becoming more fierce. You won't spend so much time on the ground, with dirty scraped up knees. You will run once more. You will find your smile. It won't happen in moments; but only over miles. You will celebrate these milestones. And the fear of letting go of all the pain, will slowly begin to dissipate. And you won't be so scared, to be known. You won't be so closed off to the possibility, that maybe just maybe, you aren't alone. Every person is battered, in their own damn way; all searching for the same answers; all trying to end up in the same place. It's all just a circle. A cyclical cycle. You're not forever trapped, in one space. Your heart has a way of doing this to you; of planting lies inside your brain. You have to fight this darkness, with everything you've got. You have to keep working through the fear, and the pain. Keep digging up your fears, and your shame. Unearth them. Hold them close. Hug them, and smash them to smithereens. For you are not bound to these lies that they told you. You don't have to live like an empty shell. You are so much more than they said you could be. They wanted you to stay face down in the dirt; in that place where they

buried you alive. But you must find your fierceness. I know
it's still there. It's just buried somewhere much deeper inside.
Please Little One. It is time for you to rise. Pick yourself up,
and find a safe place to cry. Find safe arms to hold you. Find
souls who can understand why. Find those who see what's
behind your silence, and remind you that this will get better
with time. It's time to accept your reality. It is time to own all
of the horror in your story. You will feel like you're breaking.
It won't kill you, but it should. Your world will feel like it's
shattered, but that's just the beginning. Things will get so
much better, than you ever thought they would. I cannot do it
for you. Oh how I wish that I could. Accept this space that
you're in, in this moment. Choose to love yourself, through
the pain. The sun will rise; it will come out again. You will
have more and more days, without rain. You will have more
and more moments, without feeling this heavy weight. Joy. It
used to be so elusive for a girl like me; until I woke up one
fateful morning, and decided it was time to allow myself to
dream. I found you; my joy. I felt you; my laughter. I realized
it's ok, to not have lived a fairytale. Not everyone grows up, in
happily ever after. There is no such thing, as fully leaving this
pain behind. But I got so much better, at holding onto my
smile. And slowly but surely, those steps became miles. Oh
joy, how I crave your feeling. How my heart aches on bad
days, for your healing. My bones still sometimes shiver, cause
they often don't know what to do. But I've accepted my story,
and the reality of this circle. And I know that at some point, I
will circle back to you."

-Little girl speak

Little girl speak

Rise

"Home. They say it's where the heart is. I say it's where the
heart turns cold. Shut off, forcibly cut off to preserve what is
left of itself, so it still has the time, to grow old. Giving more
space, for time to unfold. New memories made. Past secrets
retold. It's rinse and repeat, over and over again. The weight
of their sins, never lighter with time. I write poem after poem;
rhyme after rhyme. And nothing enables me, to escape this
prison. Am I containing this monster inside, or is it containing
me? These are the things that I wonder at night, when I lay my
head down, and try to sleep. Hoping. Wishing. Praying. Weep-
ing. Tossing and turning, but never ever sleeping. I have to be
put down, to shut my eyes. A pill and a glass of water, as these
feelings seem to subside. I've found my ways to avoid them.
I've perfected this skill over time. But nothing in the world is
as dangerous a poison, than ignoring the truth in your own
mind. Eventually yourself and this truth, will collide. And you
will have to make the choice to move forward, or to let yourself fall behind. It's never been about letting go. I've been lying to myself, all this time. It's about living in my truth, and
accepting who I am. It's about finding the strength, not to
hide. No matter how many graves I've let them bury me in;
this war isn't over, till I rise."

-Little girl speak

Little girl speak

Phoenix

She stands alone.
The world around her, is screaming.
She is pulled
In every direction,
Yet tethered
To where she stands;
Like concrete.
She is unmovable;
Unshakeable;
Soft in her heart,
Yet somehow, unbreakable.
She has seen underground valleys,
As cold and as black as night.
But somehow
She always ends up
On the surface,
Speaking her truth,
And fighting for what's right.
Her heart
Has been bandaged,
From a thousand bruised spaces.
And what she couldn't fix,
She wrote out
On these pages.
She is such a mystery,
Of darkness and of light.
She can be the comfort
That you seek,
Or what keeps you awake
At night.
The fire around her;

cont...

Little girl speak

It scorched her every limb,
But she clawed her way out,
And came back to life again.
Reborn from the ashes;
She fought the fiercest fight.
She taught herself
To rise again,
And with her wings;
Took flight.

-Little girl speak

Little girl speak

Songbird

She breathes in deeply,
And lets it all go;
The heaviness
Inside her wings,
As she's taken away
In the undertow.
The current beneath her,
Of flowing winds;
They beckon her
To new heights
Of strength,
Where she can master
Her demons;
Where she can learn the art
Of starting over;
Where she can rise,
And begin again.
This body she inhabits;
It only contains one life.
But in her mind
And in her soul,
She has died
And been reborn,
Many times.
She was not born fearless.
She was not born brave.
It was her early circumstances,
That caused her attributes
To change.
She became a fighter,
Very early on in life.

cont...

Little girl speak

.

She became a fierce protector,
Inside a little girl's mind.
Though she was small and tiny,
Her ability to endure the pain,
Made her mighty.
She possessed the strength and maturity
Of a woman,
Inside a child's body.
She grew her own wings,
And taught herself to fly.
And she learned something more about herself,
Every single time that she tried.
With each descent,
She broke open further;
Expelling the poison and pain,
From inside her.
And with every ascent,
She took to the sky;
Spreading her wings
A little further each time.
She is slowly stepping
Into her destiny;
Into the sacred fullness,
Of her authenticity.
She has laid there in the darkness,
Like a Phoenix with broken wings.
But even in the shadows,
A bird will always sing.
She will always remember what it felt like,
To be forced to be a woman,
When she was just a kid.
But her warrior spirit and her bravery,
Are the things she has chosen to take away from it.

cont...

Little girl speak

The world will continue to swirl all around her,
And there will always be those,
Who could never understand her.
She has a strength and a power inside her,
That is not really meant to be fully understood.
And the only ones who are able to comprehend it,
Are the only ones strong enough, who should.
She will never be as soft as some,
But she is still a sweet soul
Who is made up of kindness,
And unconditional love.
She will love you,
In the fiercest way.
She will protect you,
In the shadow of her wings.
And when you shrink down
From the demons left inside you,
She will guide you
Out of the darkness,
With every song she sings…

-Little girl speak

Little girl speak

Silence

"Silence. She calls to me. She wakes me up in the middle of the night, to remind me that she's still an option. Beckoning me to close my mouth, to shut my eyes to the truth that so often invades my space. She resurrects all these feelings of fear; all these feelings of guilt, and of shame. She reminds me of a past, that I can do absolutely nothing to change. She weaves her stories of truth, and of lies. Telling me that things would go so much easier for me, if I kept all my feelings inside. Be quiet, she tells me. Shut up and sit down. Everyone will believe that you're completely insane, if you insist on speaking your truth out loud. No one wants to hear your deafening screams. They will turn up their music, to drown out the sound. So you see, there's no point in not being silent. And nothing that you say, is prolific nor profound. No one cares about your story. No one cares about your pain. No one gives a damn about this strength, that you think is locked inside you. SHUT UP I SAID. SHUT UP AND SIT DOWN. And we all know the truth; that you're still so afraid. For something called SILENCE, she has a lot to say. She isn't ever really silent at all. And through my veins she goes pumping, every waking moment of the day. She stumbles all the way through me, though she doesn't know the way. All the ways in which she's made me feel lost. All the times she's suffocated the words inside my throat. Every time that she calls to me, I want to believe her. But something inside of me, says DON'T. I believe in the STRENGTH, that I cultivated out of darkness. I believe in this FIERCENESS, that l have woven out of pain. And when I am standing at the end of this journey, it will not be silence, that remains."

-Little girl speak

Little girl speak

The bravest of women
All over the world,
Uniting as one;
An army of girls.
Their voices
Once silent;
Diminished, and quiet.
It is hard now,
To silence the roar,
Of our riot.
Not ever again;
NO!
We will NOT
Be silent.
We will NOT
Shrink down.
We will NOT
Be quiet.
You will squirm
At the thought
Of what we've been through.
And you can thank
Your lucky stars
If you are lucky enough,
To be able to say,
That it never happened
To you.
The nightmare
We lived;
The things
We survived.

cont...

Little girl speak

Some days,
The pain still cuts me so deep,
That I am barely able
To open my eyes;
Let alone
Have the bravery,
To not run and hide;
The strength
To let anyone
See beyond my walls;
To view the horror,
Of what's still left inside.
What will it take?
How many
Of these stories
Still need to be told,
Before people get it?
Before this world
Is alive, and WOKE?
Those of us
Who have suffered;
Our eyes
Have never been closed.
We've been forced
To keep them open;
Many of us,
Since only four or five years old.
And we always carry
These memories with us;
The nightmares and the shame.
And for so very many of us,
We were told,
That we were to blame.

cont...

Little girl speak

It's hard to describe this pain
That I feel.
Hearing all these stories;
It truly is the worst kind of surreal.
To be able to comfort
And validate each other;
To know deep down,
That we are truly not alone.
Yet still wishing somehow,
It never happened to another;
Not to any girl or woman;
Not to any daughter or mother.
My bones are aching.
My knees are shaking.
My voice is cracking,
But I will keep on speaking;
As my tears
Continue to flow like a river,
From the very core, of my being.
We are safe here,
In each other's stories.
We are lovingly cradled,
As we link
Arm in arm;
As we begin to connect;
Shattered heart, to shattered heart.
As we reach out,
For each other's hand.
We are warriors,
And we are mighty.
We are a force
To be reckoned with;
No longer will our pain,

cont...

Little girl speak

Be taken so lightly.
You never know the power,
Of what sharing your story can do.
And although we are stronger
As we all band together,
My heart is still broken,
Over every, "#MeToo"

-Little girl speak

Little girl speak

She's Still Running The Show:

"Some mornings when I wake up, I can immediately feel her, in not so subtle ways. Her fears, her anxieties; Her worries. But on other days, her presence can be more subtle; just a small thought, or a ping of nervousness, or a wave of strong emotion. But ultimately what I have surmised; what I know deep down to be true, is that she, is still running the show. This petulant, persistent, terrified little girl inside of me, is still running my life. As her fragile little world collides with mine, I am forced once again, to choose. Who am I going to be, to-day? Am I her, or am I me? Now don't get me wrong. She's an adorable, little gangly thing. She has the sweetest smile, and the most adorable laugh. And her nose, is as cute as a button. And she deserves to feel very ounce of petulance, she has. She didn't have it easy, that much is for certain. She was abused, and neglected, and forgotten; tossed aside many times, like a dirty dish rag. She had to find ways to survive inside her skin; ways to survive and cope, with unimaginable terror and abuse. And you know what? She did a pretty good job, for a little girl. She survived long enough, to become me. And considering what she's been through, I applaud her. I give her a re-sounding thank you, and a standing ovation, for her tenacity. She survived things, that most adults would not. And no mat-ter how she got me here, to the middle arena of 36 years old; I'm here. And I am here, thanks to her. I literally owe her my life. But my reality, is not hers. And if I continue to live as if it is, I am going to lose very important relationships, and the re-spect of my colleagues, and my peers. There is no place for a scared little girl, in my work environment. There is no place for a neglected child, in my friendships. And there is no place for an angry little girl, in my romantic relationship. I want; even need, to keep her sensitivity that she has toward others; her empathy, her compassion, her warm, and caring nature.

Little girl speak

But her survival mode has got to go, because it's literally killing me. She's like a toddler who's running around, just putting her hands on everything. And I'm chasing after her, but I'm tired; I'm exhausted and exasperated, and she can run so much faster than me. I can't keep up with her, no matter how hard I try. And she keeps spilling things all over the place, and throwing things everywhere. And as I survey the spaces around me, she's creating such clutter. She is making quite a mess, of my world. In the beginning, I felt guilty stopping her. After all, she had never been allowed to speak her mind. She had never been allowed to be sad, or angry, or outraged over the horrific things that were done to her. So I let her run wild. I let her scream, and rant. I let her cry, and throw tantrums. Now, anyone who has ever taken care of a child knows, that sometimes you have to pick your battles. Sometimes, you just have to let them throw their hissy fit, and clean up the mess afterwards. But this was not a five minute temper tantrum. This was not some clutter on a toy room floor, that you could quickly pick up after. I am standing in the midst, of utter devastation and destruction here. The damage I allowed her to do, and the mess that's left behind in her wake, is massive. I am sitting here on the ground, amidst piles of rubble. And I, am spent. I am completely, and utterly exhausted. And as I look up, she's still running in circles. She's still going; throwing things around, and jumping up and down in anger; pouncing on piles of junk, strewn across the ruins I've allowed her to create. And then, it happens. Out of the corner of her little eyes, she sees me in her peripheral. And something begins to shift, inside of her. Her anxiety, begins to quiet down. Her rage, comes to a screeching halt, as confusion spreads across her face. I am no longer standing there, applauding her efforts. I am no longer her captive audience. I'm just an exhausted woman, sitting in the junk heap, of what's left of my life. And slowly; very slowly she walks up to me, and stares deeply into my eyes. Tilting her head, in confusion. Pulling my eyelids open further, to make sure that I am still awake, and that I can still see her. She places her little hands on my cheeks, and she nods, as if she understands. And then she wraps her arms tightly around me, and whispers in my ear: "thank you." You see, nobody ever let her feel anything. No one ever allowed her, to let it out; any of it. So there I sat, with this little girl's arms draped around my neck, and tears streaming down her face, and onto the back of my shirt; knowing, that I had done the right thing, for her. But sitting there, surveying the damage that it had done to my life? To my world? I breathed in deeply, and let out a very soft sigh, and whispered to her: "it's alright." And somehow in that moment, we both knew that it would be. But she knew just as much as I did, that I couldn't let her run the show anymore. Her story is a part of mine, but it can't be my future. And it certainly cannot be the basis for how I live my life, or the ways in which I move through my world any- more. I used to think that choosing to stop any emotions that she felt, was stifling her; that it wasn't fair to her; that it was wrong of me, to even think about doing so, after she was kept tortured and silent for so long. But I let her have her rant. I let her kick and scream. I let her have her reign of justice. And continuing to allow a little girl, to run a woman's life, is just plain irresponsible. And this unspoken truth between us; be- tween me and her, was realized that day, as we embraced amongst the rubble. This process of transition; this process of the adult me, taking over my own life, has been an uphill climb at best. It's been scary and confusing, and extremely painful. There have been many days, when I feel her anger teaming beneath the surface. Something triggers her sadness, and I become reactive, and undone. But it is not me who is reacting in those moments, it is her; it's that beautifully stub- born little girl, with pigtails. But she doesn't look so cute when she's angry. And when she cries, it still breaks my heart.

I think it always will. And that's ok. It's ok for her sadness, to break my heart. It's ok for her anger, and her feelings of injustice, to rattle and stir inside of me, from time to time. But I can no longer base my decisions, and reactions, on how she feels. Making this conscious daily decision several times a day, to run my own life, is a new concept for me. Some days, it's pretty easy. But other days, it's extremely difficult. But I know deep down, that I am doing the right thing now, for myself and for her, by taking over. She can't run the show anymore. But that doesn't mean, that I don't still see her. It doesn't mean, that I don't still love her, and value her feelings. It just means that it's time to handle my emotions, and relate to my world as an adult. And writing pieces like this one, and going out into the world, trying to find others like her who I can love well; finding those broken souls, that I can love back to life; that, is what makes her smile these days. That, is how I love her. That, is how I honor her pain, and her story. Giving her the space she needed to let it all out, was me validating her reality. But not allowing her to run my life anymore, was the smartest decision I have ever made, for the both of us."

-Little girl speak

A closing letter to you, beautiful survivor

Dear survivor,

I want you to know, that I love you. I want you to know, that I see you. Your pain, is not invisible to me. You matter. Your story matters. Your heartache matters. Your joy matters. Your hope matters. Your sadness matters. Your laughter matters. I know the path that is set before you. I could tell you every twist and turn, with my eyes closed. I know that your path will not be completely identical to mine, but I know it will be similar. And if I can survive my healing, so can you. I know how that you're scared. It's ok to be afraid, but you can do this. And I want you to know, that you're not alone. I am right here, fighting alongside you; for your continued freedom, and my own.

Love,

Sarah

Sarah Kacala

About the Author

Sarah Kacala lives in Pennsylvania with her husband and their two children. Writing has been a huge part of her life, for as far back as she can remember. Her advocacy work with survivors is her biggest passion. She made the decision to channel her writing into empowering and inspiring other survivors like herself, to begin to find their voice again, and to begin to heal.

Social Media

Facebook
https://www.facebook.com/littlegirlspeak/

Printed in Great Britain
by Amazon